Name

Ahmed

Class

Class 4,5,6

Teacher

ostard ya

01

Rules of Tajwīd

Fourth edition, 2018

Part of the Safar Learn to Read Series

Published by

Safar Publications, London, England

www.safarpublications.org

support@safarpublications.org

ISBN 978-1-912437-24-5

A catalogue record for this book is available from the British Library.

Printed in Turkey

Rules of
Tajwīd

Contents

Introduction

Safar Rules of Tajwīd is part of the Safar Learn to Read Series and a sequel to the Safar Qāʿidah. Rules of Tajwīd consists of seven progressive levels that follow on from the 13 levels of the Safar Qāʿidah. This book may be taught alongside Juz ʿAmma or once the student has started to read the Qurʾān. While teaching this book, it is essential that one is familiar with the 13 levels in the *Qāʿidah* and that the student's firm grip on the 13 levels does not deteriorate or become weak.

Those who are aware of *Tajwīd* taught in the traditional method will notice that there is a difference to the order in which rules appear in this book. However, for the past decade, we have implemented a number of methods in teaching *Tajwīd* rules to our students. Teachers were able to devise their own methods and these were trialled and re-trialled with tweaks for several years. Our aim was to make learning easy, especially for those who may find difficulty in learning and recalling rules of this kind, which meant that some restructuring of certain rules was necessary. Finally, the most effective methods that bore the greatest results have been brought together in this book.

In some places, we have avoided exceptions to rules in favour of explaining them in the forthcoming advanced *Tajwīd* book. For example, exceptions to the rules of *Rā Sākinah* have not been mentioned in Level 17c as, in our experience, students find it difficult to comprehend them at this stage. Furthermore, we have tried to ensure that examples of exceptions do not occur in this book, other than the word "*al-dunyā*" (الدُّنْيَا), due to the exceptionally high occurrence of the word in the Qurʾān.

In the same method as the Safar Qāʿidah, a student will master one rule at a time. The difference in this book, however, is that a student will have to demonstrate their ability to spot the rules before reading the examples from the Qurʾān to the teacher.

To further explain this, the method of learning will be:

1. A student must first understand the rule from the book.

2. All the paragraphs accompanied by a heart symbol must be memorised word-by-word and then revised and retained throughout the course of learning *Tajwīd*.

3. Thereafter, he will spot the rules he has so far covered in the section the teacher assigns as homework. Every time he sees an occurrence of a rule, he will say the exact wording found under the "Spot the rule" header at the bottom of the first page of the level. In some traditional learning systems, this method is known as *Ijrāʾ*.

4. Once the teacher thinks the student has become proficient in spotting a certain rule, in order to save time, he can allow the student to use a shorter, abbreviated sentence for that rule.

Homework for a student will not only be to read a passage to the teacher every lesson but to be able to *spot the rules* efficiently too. This will require a considerable amount of time each week till each new rule is mastered.

How long each rule will take to master will depend on a few variables: the retention-ability of a student, the frequency of revisiting each rule, and - most importantly - the standard to which the student completes his homework. In mastering *Tajwīd*, the theory makes up five percent, as opposed to its practice which makes up ninety-five percent. For a student to recite the Qur'ān with a high level of *Tajwīd*, it is vital that he repeats the passage over and over again.

It should be noted that most students at this stage feel it is unnecessary to do this when they are able to read the passage with fluency after practicing it a few times. However, it is not the fluency of recitation that is the learning objective here but the quality of *Tajwīd* within the recitation. It is far better for a student to read a few chapters of the Qur'ān with good quality *Tajwīd* than to finish the entire Qur'ān with poor *Tajwīd*. The former will be able to read the rest of the Qur'ān correctly without the supervision of a teacher while the latter will continue to make mistakes even with the aid of a teacher.

Both parents and teachers need to direct the student to this learning objective by ensuring that the student practices the set homework (of the Qur'ān) repeatedly in a slow and steady manner. It is recommended that the set passage does not exceed a page and that it is recited 25-40 times over before reading to the teacher. Students at Safar Academy, who have maintained this, alḥamdulillah, have become competent in reciting the Qur'ān with *Tajwīd* within the space of two to three years.

The exercises in this book do not appear in colour-coded writing for the simple reason that one who learns through the aid of colours finds it difficult to read a black and white Qur'ān with *Tajwīd*. The pages of this book have not been laminated so that appropriate markings can be made by the teacher where necessary.

We are extremely grateful to our esteemed Ustādh Mawlāna Yusuf Darwan (May Allāh bless and reward him!) for his continued support and advice, and for guiding us towards a decision whenever complex issues of *Tajwīd* came to light.

Special thanks go to Muhi Uddin who supervised most of the work in this book, and to Ishaq Ganee and Hussain Ahmed for their continuous advice. Thanks also go to Maaz Patel, Ismail Jeilani and Hamza Ahmad Khan for working on various aspects of the book and Reedwan Iqbal for its design. I thank all other members of our staff, who have helped to bring this work to this stage, many of whom will go unmentioned but whose reward is with Allāh the Almighty.

Finally, we thank Allāh ﷾ for giving us this opportunity to serve His *dīn* and pray that He makes the work a true success in both worlds for all those who use it. We ask the reader to pray for us and all those who have contributed to this work, both academically and financially.

Your brother in Islam

Hasan Ali, MA Education (Psychology)

4 May 2015/ 15 Rajab 1436

Ādāb of the Qur'ān

The one who intends to read the Qur'ān or learn *Tajwīd* should do so to seek the pleasure of Allāh ﷾ alone. The Prophet ﷺ has said, "Whoever seeks such knowledge that should be used to seek Allāh's pleasure, but (instead) uses it to seek a worldly gain, will not smell the fragrance of Paradise on the Day of Judgement".[1] Sincerity should be at the core of one's studies, for the Prophet ﷺ has said "Actions are determined by intentions".[2] This means that, by learning the Qur'ān, one should not seek the praise or love of people; wealth or position; superiority over one's peers or fame; or to gain anything but the pleasure of Allāh ﷾. One should also not leave the recitation of the Qur'ān out of fear of this, for some of our pious predecessors have said, "We sought knowledge for [reasons] other than [pleasing] Allāh ﷾ but eventually it all became for the sake of Allāh ﷾".

It is obligatory for a Muslim to revere the Qur'ān and this is done in many ways. The greatest is to believe in every letter of the Qur'ān; denying even a letter of it will take one out of the fold of Islām. Even making a joke about the Qur'ān is a serious offence, which may result in one losing his faith. Another way of revering the Qur'ān is to keep it away from any place of filth and to not touch it without *wuḍū'*. It was the habit of the early predecessors to handle it with great care and, when putting it away, to place it somewhere high. Another important way of revering it is to act upon its message.

[1] Abū Dāwūd: 3664; [2] Bukhārī: 1

It is important that a student remains humble in the presence of his teacher and is respectful to him and others who are in his gathering. The greeting of *Salām* should be given to him first before greeting others. The student should sit in front of him in a manner that is befitting of a student and not a teacher, displaying an eagerness to learn; he should not raise his voice above that of the teacher; he should not speak more than what is required; he should not be fidgety or inattentive but accept the good advice the teacher offers. One should not point his finger while speaking to his teacher; beckon him with his eyes; interrupt him while he speaks or speak ill of others in front of him. Rather, one should seek to benefit from him and tolerate any hardship in learning. When the teacher is leaving one should say *Salām* to him once again.

As for one's peers, a student should neither become jealous of what Allāh ﷻ has given to another nor should he feel a sense of pride over others. Rather, he should remind himself that every skill obtained is only through the bounty of Allāh ﷻ. To combat jealousy, one should see every gift or skill in a person as the result of Allāh's ﷻ wisdom and, therefore, should not show a disliking for what Allāh ﷻ has willed.

When sitting to read the Qur'ān one should perform *wuḍū'*, clean his mouth with a *siwāk*, pray two *rak'ahs* of *Ṣalāh*– whether he is in the *masjid* or not – and then sit in a clean place, with great respect for the Qur'ān, facing the *Qiblah* (if possible). Then he should proceed by saying *Ta'awwudh* and *Basmalah* before reciting. One should not fidget or look around unnecessarily but imagine he is having a secret conversation with Allāh ﷻ or that Allāh ﷻ is watching him while he recites.

He should then try to concentrate and ponder over what he is reading, for this is the real remedy of the heart. Allāh ﷻ has said, "A blessed book We have revealed to you, so that they may ponder over its verses".[3] Some of our pious predecessors would spend an entire night reciting the same verse and pondering over its meaning. One should try and cry or at least express fear when reaching verses regarding the wrath of Allāh. But such crying or fear should not lead to showing off one's deeds to others (riyā'). It is better to recite loudly than to recite quietly – if one does not fear riyā' – otherwise to recite quietly is better. It is also more virtuous to recite the Qur'ān in a beautiful tune.

The Qur'ān should not be recited in a dirty place or where there are great distractions. Even when passing wind or yawning one should stop reciting until he finishes passing wind or yawning. One should not disturb a person reciting the Qur'ān, even by saying salām to him, for he is communicating with Allāh ﷻ. And when coming across a *sajdah* of *tilāwah*, one should perform it immediately or at the earliest convenience.

One may recite the Qur'ān at anytime but the recitation in the depth of the night is always better than any other time, as this is the time Allāh ﷻ is closest to His servants. As for the day, the best time to read it is at *Fajr*, as this is the time when angels witness one's recitation.[4]

A student should try and keep his heart clean from those things that Allāh ﷻ has prohibited, so that the heart can be receptive to the Qur'ān, for the Prophet has said, "Beware! In the body there is a morsel of flesh, when it is intact the whole body is intact and when it is corrupt the whole body is corrupt. Remember this [morsel of flesh] is the heart!"[5]

[3] Sūrah Ṣād 38:29; [4] Sūrah Isrā' 17:78; [5] Muslim: 1599

One should take advantage of having time to learn before one becomes occupied, for 'Umar ﷺ said, "gain a deep understanding of the religion before you are given responsibilities", because the older a person becomes the less time he will have to learn the religion.

A student should know that the recitation of the Qur'ān is one of the most rewarding actions in Islām and a great means of coming closer to Allāh ﷻ. One should recite it daily and aim to finish a Qur'ān every month (as was the practice of many *Ṣaḥābah*) or, if not possible, every two months (as was the practice of many pious predecessors). *Du'a's* are accepted at the time when one finishes the Qur'ān and there are a few authentic narrations where the *Ṣaḥābah* called one another to witness such an occasion and made *du'ā'*.

Extracted from Imām Nawawi's *Al-Tibyān fī Ādābī Ḥamalat al-Qur'ān* with minor changes.

How to use this book

To take most benefit from the book, all its features should be used to their full. Below is an explanation for various elements. Ultimately, it is up to the teacher and the institute which of these elements are used and how. It is imperative that the teacher, management, student and parents all understand how each one is being used in their setting. Parents should ask the teacher if in any doubt.

Due and pass ticks

In the border of each page, in line with the exercises, there are outlines for ticks. The first portion of the tick - the smaller portion - should be marked for the lines that the teacher wishes to set as homework. Once the student reads the homework to the teacher, the teacher can complete the ticks for the lines the student has passed. if there are any lines that the student does not pass, the first portion will remain. In the example on the right, the student has passed the top line but not the bottom one. The teacher may also use the empty space between the margin and text to write the date the homework is due and when the student passes. As an example, we have used "D:" for the date the homework was due and "P:" for the date the student passed. If the student passes on the due-date, the tick will suffice and a seperate pass-date will not be required.

D: 22-9
P: 27-9

D: 28-9

Correction code

When the student makes a mistake, the teacher may
wish to make a record of what type of mistake was
made. Most major mistakes fall into six categories
and we have given each a letter:

MISTAKE KEY
STRETCH
LETTER
FLUENCY
JOIN
HARAKAH
يَسْعَى
PRONUNCIATION

- **L (Letter):** if the student reads the wrong
  letter; for example ش in place of س, or makes
  a mistake in letter recognition.

- **P (Pronunciation):** if he pronounces a letter incorrectly.

- **F (Fluency):** if he does not read fluently enough.

- **H (Ḥarakah):** if the wrong *ḥarakah* is read.

- **S (Stretch):** this covers two types of mistake: if they stretch a normal
  ḥarakah, or forget to stretch one of the six stretched *ḥarakahs*.

- **J (Joining):** if a mistake is made whilst joining one letter or word to
  another where there is a *sukūn* or *shaddah*.

The first time a student makes a mistake, the teacher may decide not to
make a mark. If the same mistake is made again, a line or a circle may be
drawn. If made for the third time, the marking code may be used. If the
student still persists, a comment may be written in the white space around
the exercise. Please see the example in the "Comments" section below.

Homework diary

TIME (MIN)	MON	TUE	WED	THU	FRI	SAT	SUN	PARENT INITIALS	PASS STAMP	21-9-13	START DATE
WEEK 1 ▶	20	15	20	20	25	30	30	HA	MMU	28-9-13	PASS DATE
WEEK 2 ▶											

The date for the commencing week should be written in the first column to the left. Thereafter, under each day, the parents can record how much the student practiced. This can be done in two ways: by writing how many minutes they spent practicing, or how many times they revised the homework. It is up to the teacher which method he prefers and he should make this clear to the students and parents from the outset. On the right hand side, the teacher may wish to write the date the page was started and then completed. Also, the teacher may place a sticker, use a stamp or sign in the "Pass Stamp" section.

Comments

Comments can be made in the column labelled "Notes". An indicator should be used to show which word or line the comment relates to.

The rules at a glance

14 LEVEL

14 Ta'awwudh and Basmalah

Very important to say ?

♥ **Ta'awwudh** (تَعَوُّذ) **means:**
to say "أَعُوْذُ بِاللّٰهِ مِنَ الشَّيْطٰنِ الرَّجِيْمِ".
By saying this, I seek Allāh's (سبحانه وتعالى)
protection from Shayṭān, the rejected.

♥ **Basmalah** (بَسْمَلَة) **means:**
to say "بِسْمِ اللّٰهِ الرَّحْمٰنِ الرَّحِيْمِ".
By saying this, I ask Allāh's (سبحانه وتعالى) help and
blessings.

♥ **The rule is:**
that I should say both of these before
reciting the Qur'ān. If there is an
interruption in my recitation, I should
repeat *Ta'awwudh*.

أَعُوْذُ بِاللهِ مِنَ الشَّيْطٰنِ الرَّجِيْمِ ○

(I seek Allāh's protection from Shayṭān, the rejected.)

بِسْمِ اللهِ الرَّحْمٰنِ الرَّحِيْمِ ○

(With Allāh's name, the Most Merciful, the Most Kind.)

HOMEWORK KEY	TIME (MIN)	MON	TUE	WED	THU	FRI	SAT	SUN	PARENT INITIALS	PASS STAMP	START DATE
✓ DUE	WEEK 1										PASS DATE
✓ PASS	WEEK 2										

Jundub ibn 'Abd Allāh ﵁ *says,*

"We were with the Prophet ﷺ *as boys approaching our teens. We learnt Īmān before we learnt the Qur'ān and then we learnt the Qur'ān and it increased us in Īmān."*

(Ibn Mājah: 61)

15

LEVEL

15 Mīm Mushaddadah (مِيم مُشَلَّدَة)
and Nūn Mushaddadah (نُون مُشَلَّدَة)

So far, I can apply the rules of:

 Ta'awwudh and *Basmalah*

♥ **Ghunnah** (غُنَّة) **means:**
for the sound to come out from the nose for the duration of 2 ḥarakahs.

♥ **The rule is:**
that I will always read Mīm *Mushaddadah* and Nūn *Mushaddadah* with *ghunnah*.

♥ **For example:**

ثُمَّ , اِنَّ

Spot the rule

 Every time I see this rule, I will say:
"Mīm *Mushaddadah, ghunnah*"
or "Nūn *Mushaddadah, ghunnah*."

NOTES

اِنَّمَا ◄ وَاُمِّهٖ ◄ لَيُخْرَجَنَّ ◄ فَاِتَّمَاهِىَ ◄ اِنَّهُ ظَنَّ ⁵ ⁴ ³ ² ¹

اِنَّهُ طَغٰى ◌ ◄ فَاَمْسِكُوْهُنَّ ◄ فَنِعِمَّاهِىَ ◄ ثُمَّ يُقَالُ ⁹ ⁸ ⁷ ⁶

لَتُؤْمِنُنَّ بِهٖ ◄ اَنَّ شِئْتُمْ ◄ وَاعْفُ عَنَّا ◄ حَتّٰى ¹³ ¹² ¹¹ ¹⁰

يُؤْمِنَّ ◄ كَمَثَلِ جَنَّةٍ ◄ وَمَتِّعُوْهُنَّ ◄ فَحَسْبَهٗ ¹⁶ ¹⁵ ¹⁴

جَهَنَّمُ ◄ وَجَنّٰتٍ اَلْفَافًا ◌ ◄ ثُمَّ اَحْيَاهُمْ ◄ وَهٰذَا ¹⁹ ¹⁸ ¹⁷

النَّبِىُّ ◄ وَمَنَافِعُ لِلنَّاسِ ◄ ثُمَّ بَعَثَهٗ ◄ هُنَّ اُمُّ ²² ²¹ ²⁰

الْكِتٰبِ ◄ وَاَتِمُّوا الْحَجَّ وَالْعُمْرَةَ ◄ لَمْ يَتَسَنَّهْ ◄ اَنّٰى ²⁵ ²⁴ ²³

يُحْىٖ هٰذِهٖ ◄ لَاَمْلَئَنَّ جَهَنَّمَ ◄ وَلَا تُسْمِعُ الصُّمَّ ²⁷ ²⁶

وَالنّٰشِطٰتِ نَشْطًا ◌ ◄ وَسَيُجَنَّبُهَا الْاَتْقَى ◌ ◄ ظَنَّ ³⁰ ²⁹ ²⁸

الْجَاهِلِيَّةِ ◄ فَلَمَّا نَجّٰهُمْ ◄ وَلَا يَصُدَّنَّكُمُ الشَّيْطٰنُ ³² ³¹

اِنَّ عَلَيْنَا لَلْهُدٰى ◌ ◄ لَمَّا عَلَيْهَا حَافِظٌ ◄ اِنَّهُمْ ³⁵ ³⁴ ³³

يَكِيْدُوْنَ كَيْدًا ◌ ◄ فَاَمَّا مَنْ اَعْطٰى ◄ اِنَّ مَثَلَ ³⁷ ³⁶

عِيْسٰى ◄ وَاِذَا الْجَنَّةُ اُزْلِفَتْ ◌ ◄ ءَاِذَا كُنَّا عِظَامًا ³⁹ ³⁸

HOMEWORK KEY		TIME (MIN)	MON	TUE	WED	THU	FRI	SAT	SUN	PARENT INITIALS	PASS STAMP		START DATE
✓	DUE	WEEK 1 ►									★		PASS DATE
✓	PASS	WEEK 2 ►											

NOTES

فَلَهَا ◀ فَتَيَمَّمُوا۟ صَعِيدًا ◌ۢ ◀ وَيَتَجَنَّبُهَا الْأَشْقَى
1 . 2 . 3

الثُّلُثُ ◌ۘ ◀ فَلِأُمِّهِ ◀ يَعِدُهُمْ وَيُمَنِّيهِمْ ◀ النِّصْفُ ◌ۗ
4 . 5

وَنَهَى النَّفْسَ ◀ وَأَمَّا مَنْ خَافَ ◀ يَوْمَ يَقُومُ النَّاسُ
6 . 7 . 8

فَإِنَّ الْجَحِيمَ ◀ وَإِذَا النُّفُوسُ زُوِّجَتْ ◌ۙ ◀ عَنِ الْهَوَى ◌ۙ
9 . 10

وَلَأُنتُمَّ ◀ فَإِنَّ الْجَنَّةَ هِيَ الْمَأْوَى ◌ۚ ◀ هِيَ الْمَأْوَى ◌ۚ
11 . 12

مِنْ أَمْوَالِ ◀ لِيَحْكُمَ بَيْنَ النَّاسِ ◀ نِعْمَتِي عَلَيْكُمْ
13 . 14

أَنَّى يَكُونُ لِي ◀ هُنَّ لِبَاسٌ لَكُمْ ◌ۚ ◀ النَّاسِ
15 . 16

إِنَّكَ جَامِعُ النَّاسِ ◀ فَإِنَّكَ لَا تُسْمِعُ الْمَوْتَى ◀ غُلَامٌ
17 . 18

إِنَّ فِي ◀ فِي جَنَّةٍ عَالِيَةٍ ◌ۙ ◀ إِنَّ لِلْمُتَّقِينَ مَفَازًا ◌ۙ
19 . 20 . 21

بَيَّنَّا لَكُمُ الْآيَتِ ◀ إِذَا بَلَغُوا۟ النِّكَاحَ ◀ ذَلِكَ
22 . 23

قُلْتُمْ أَنَّ ◀ أَمَّا مَنِ اسْتَغْنَى ◀ إِنَّنَا سَمِعْنَا مُنَادِيًا
24 . 25 . 26

وَهَنًّا ◀ حَمَلَتْهُ أُمُّهُ ◀ يَسْتَخْفُونَ مِنَ النَّاسِ ◀ هَذَا
27 . 28

وَلَا تَحْسَبَنَّ الَّذِينَ قُتِلُوا۟ ◀ لِتَحْكُمَ بَيْنَ النَّاسِ
29 . 30

NOTES

1 ثُمَّ إِنَّ عَلَيْنَا حِسَابَهُمْ ○ ◄ 2 ثُمَّ سَوّٰىهُ وَنَفَخَ فِيْهِ ◄

3 إِنَّ هٰذَا لَفِي الصُّحُفِ الْأُوْلٰى ◄ 4 وَلَا تَيَمَّمُوا الْخَبِيْثَ

مِنْهُ ◄ 5 فَإِنَّمَا عَلَيْكَ الْبَلٰغُ ط ◄ 6 فَإِنَّمَا يَقُوْلُ

لَهٗ كُنْ ◄ 7 الْكِتٰبَ وَالْحُكْمَ وَالنُّبُوَّةَ ◄ 8 ثُمَّ اَتِمُّوا

الصِّيَامَ إِلَى الَّيْلِ ج ◄ 9 ثُمَّ لَا يَمُوْتُ فِيْهَا وَلَا يَحْيٰى ○ط ◄

10 فَإِنَّمَا يَكْسِبُهٗ عَلٰى نَفْسِهٖ ط ◄ 11 نُوَلِّهٖ مَا تَوَلّٰى وَنُصْلِهٖ

جَهَنَّمَ ط ◄ 12 فَبَلَغْنَ اَجَلَهُنَّ فَلَا تَعْضُلُوْهُنَّ ◄

13 إِنَّ يَوْمَ الْفَصْلِ كَانَ مِيْقَاتًا ○لا ◄ 14 وَإِذَا سَاَلَكَ عِبَادِيْ

عَنِّيْ ◄ 15 لِئَلَّا يَكُوْنَ لِلنَّاسِ عَلَيْكُمْ حُجَّةٌ قلا ◄

16 لَتُبَيِّنُنَّهٗ لِلنَّاسِ وَلَا تَكْتُمُوْنَهٗ ز ◄ 17 ثُمَّ اَفِيْضُوْا

مِنْ حَيْثُ اَفَاضَ النَّاسُ ◄ 18 وَالّٰتِيْ تَخَافُوْنَ

نُشُوْزَهُنَّ فَعِظُوْهُنَّ ◄ 19 فَلَمَّا جَاوَزَهٗ هُوَ وَالَّذِيْنَ

اٰمَنُوْا مَعَهٗ ◄ 20 وَتِلْكَ الْاَيَّامُ نُدَاوِلُهَا بَيْنَ النَّاسِ ◄

HOMEWORK KEY	TIME (MIN)	MON	TUE	WED	THU	FRI	SAT	SUN	PARENT INITIALS	PASS STAMP		START DATE
✓ DUE	WEEK 1											PASS DATE
✓ PASS	WEEK 2											

The Prophet ﷺ said that

it is better for you to come to the masjid and learn or recite two verses of the Qurʾān than getting two camels (for free); three verses are better than getting three camels; four verses are better than getting four camels; and [so on and so forth] for every number of verses a camel (for free).

(Muslim: 803)

16

16 Qalqalah (قَلْقَلَة)

So far, I can apply the rules of:

☑ Ta'awwudh and Basmalah

☑ Mīm Mushaddadah and Nūn Mushaddadah

♥ **Qalqalah means:**
for the sound of the letter to bounce back or echo, instead of stopping smoothly and immediately.

♥ **The rule is:**
when any of the five letters of قُطْبُ جَدٍ (ق ط ب ج د) is sākin (سَاكِن), I will read it with Qalqalah.

♥ **For example:**

أَحَدٌ○, حَبْلٌ

Note:
A common mistake is to make a small Qalqalah on the letters ل, مـ and ن.

When stopping on a Qalqalah letter it will have Qalqalah if you are making the last letter sākin. If the last letter has a shaddah on it, there will still be Qalqalah, but only after pronouncing the shaddah; for example, وَتَبَّ.

Spot the rule

Every time I see this rule, I will say:
"Qāf from قُطْبُ جَدٍ: Qalqalah."

NOTES

تُبْعَثُونَ ◄ أَخْرَجْنَا ◄ فَكَانَتْ ◄ أَبْوَابًا ۨ ◄ وَمَا

⁴ ³ ² ¹

قَدْ ◄ يُدْرِيكَ ◄ فَسَوْفَ يَدْعُوا ◄ وَالسَّبْحَتِ سَبْحًا ◄

⁷ ⁶ ⁵

بِهَذَا ◄ إِذَا وَقَبَ ۨ ◄ حَمَّالَةَ الْحَطَبِ ۙ ◄ أَفْلَحَ

¹⁰ ⁹ ⁸

الَّذِى ◄ إِذَا حَسَدَ ۨ ◄ فَالسّٰبِقٰتِ سَبْقًا ۨ ◄ الْبَلَدِ ۨ ◄

¹³ ¹² ¹¹

وَلَقَدْ خَلَقْنَا ◄ لَمُبْتَلِينَ ۝ ◄ كُنَّا ◄ خَلَقَ

¹⁵ ¹⁴

وَادْفَعُوا ◄ أَوْ تُبْدُوهُ ◄ فَاجْتَنِبُوهُ ◄ مَا اقْتَتَلُوا ◄

¹⁹ ¹⁸ ¹⁷ ¹⁶

أَيَّانَ يُبْعَثُونَ ◄ قَدْ صَدَقْتَنَا ◄ فَوَلِّ وَجْهَكَ ◄

²² ²¹ ²⁰

لِيَطْمَئِنَّ قَلْبِى ◄ ثُمَّ نَبْتَهِلْ ◄ ذٰلِكُمْ فِسْقٌ ◄

²⁵ ²⁴ ²³

فَقِنَا سُبْحٰنَكَ ◄ وَكَتَبْنَا عَلَيْهِمْ ◄ وَابْتَلُوا الْيَتٰمٰى ◄

²⁸ ²⁷ ²⁶

وَأَقْوَمُ ◄ النَّفْسُ الْمُطْمَئِنَّةُ ۨ ◄ قَوْلُهُ الْحَقُّ ◄

³¹ ³⁰ ²⁹

فَلْيَدْعُ نَادِيَهُ ۨ ◄ سَنَدْعُ الزَّبَانِيَةَ ۨ ◄ لِلشَّهَادَةِ

³³ ³²

وَثَبِّتْ ◄ النَّجْمُ الثَّاقِبُ ۨ ◄ وَخَلَقْنٰكُمْ أَزْوَاجًا ۨ ◄

³⁶ ³⁵ ³⁴

وَادْخُلِى جَنَّتِى ◄ وَالْعٰدِيٰتِ ضَبْحًا ۨ ◄ أَقْدَامَنَا

³⁸ ³⁷

NOTES

وَهَدَيْنَهُ النَّجْدَيْنِ ۛ ◄ فَقَدْ سَأَلُوا مُوسَى ◄ إِذَا

١ ٢ ٣

مَا ابْتَلَـٰهُ ◄ ادْخُلُوا فِي السِّلْمِ ◄ فَقَدْ حَبِطَ عَمَلُهُ ◄

٤ ٥

وَلَا يَخَافُ عُقْبَهَا ۛ ◄ قَالَ ٱلَيْسَ هَـٰذَا بِٱلْحَقِّ ◄

٦ ٧

يَدْعُوكَ لِيَجْزِيَكَ ◄ نَزَّلَ ٱلْكِتَـٰبَ بِٱلْحَقِّ ◄ وَلَا

٨ ٩ ١٠

جِدَالَ فِي ٱلْحَجِّ ◄ إِلَّا مَا قَدْ سَلَفَ ◄ وَٱجْتَبَيْنَٰهُمْ ◄

١١ ١٢

مِنْ أَجْلِ ذَٰلِكَ ۛ ◄ ثُمَّ شَقَقْنَا ٱلْأَرْضَ ◄ عَبْدًا إِذَا

١٣ ١٤ ١٥

صَلَّىٰ ۛ ◄ ذَٰلِكَ ٱلْيَوْمُ ٱلْحَقُّ ◄ وَٱلصُّبْحِ إِذَا تَنَفَّسَ ۛ ◄ قَد

١٨ ١٧ ١٦

ضَلَلْتُ إِذًا ◄ فَوَسَطْنَ بِهِ جَمْعًا ۛ ◄ وَٱلَّيْلِ وَمَا

١٩ ٢٠

وَسَقَ ۛ ◄ ٱلَمْ يَجِدْكَ يَتِيمًا ◄ قَدْ كَانَ لَكُمْ ءَايَةٌ ◄

٢١ ٢٢

وَلَا يَبْخَسْ مِنْهُ شَيْـًٔا ◄ مَا خَلَقْتَ هَـٰذَا بَـٰطِلًا ◄

٢٣ ٢٤

لِيَجْمَعَنَّكُمْ إِلَىٰ يَوْمِ ٱلْقِيَٰمَةِ ◄ وَأُدْخِلَ ٱلْجَنَّةَ فَقَدْ

٢٥ ٢٦

فَازَ ◄ كُلُّ شَىْءٍ هَالِكٌ إِلَّا وَجْهَهُ ◄ مِنْ أَوْسَطِ

٢٧ ٢٨

مَا تُطْعِمُونَ أَهْلِيكُمْ ◄ أَفَحُكْمَ ٱلْجَاهِلِيَّةِ يَبْغُونَ ◄

٢٩

	PASS STAMP	TIME (MIN)	MON	TUE	WED	THU	FRI	SAT	SUN	PARENT INITIALS	CORRECTION KEY
START DATE		WEEK 1 ▶									STRETCH LETTER ... JOIN HARAKA
PASS DATE		WEEK 2 ▶									يَسْعَىٰ FLUENCY ... PRONUNCIATIC

NOTES

فَلَا ◄ لِيَقْضِىَ اللهُ اَمْرًا ◄ اَلَمْ يَجْعَلْ كَيْدَهُمْ ◄
3 2 1

اقْتَحَمَ الْعَقَبَةَ ۚ ◄ لَمْ يَلِدْ ۙ ﵁ وَلَمْ يُوْلَدْ ۙ ﵁ ◄
4

حَتّٰى يَبْلُغَ الْهَدْىُ ◄ حَتّٰى يَبْلُغَ الْكِتٰبُ اَجَلَهٗ ۪ ◄
6 5

مُذَبْذَبِيْنَ ◄ وَلِنَجْعَلَكَ اٰيَةً لِّلنَّاسِ ◄ مَحِلَّهٗ ۪ ◄
8 7

اَلَمْ نَجْعَلْ ◄ لَا تَعْدُوْا فِي السَّبْتِ ۚ ◄ بَيْنَ ذٰلِكَ ۚ ◄
10 9

وَهُوَ ◄ صَدَقٰتِكُمْ ◄ لَا تُبْطِلُوْا ◄ لَّهٗ عَيْنَيْنِ ﵁ ◄
12 11

كُلِّ ◄ ثُمَّ اجْعَلْ عَلٰى ◄ يُطْعِمُ وَلَا يُطْعَمُ ◄
13

اِنَّ رَبَّكَ ◄ اِنَّ النَّاسَ قَدْ جَمَعُوْا لَكُمْ ◄ جَبَلٍ ◄
15 14

خَلَقْنٰكُمْ ◄ اَفَحَسِبْتُمْ اَنَّمَا ◄ يَقْضِىْ بَيْنَهُمْ ◄
16

حَتّٰى ◄ فَاِنْ خَرَجْنَ فَلَا جُنَاحَ عَلَيْكُمْ ◄ عَبَثًا ◄
18 17

فَتَحْنَا عَلَيْهِمْ ◄ يَتَبَيَّنَ لَكُمُ الْخَيْطُ الْاَبْيَضُ ◄
19

الَّذِىْ اَحْسَنَ ◄ وَلَنَجْزِيَنَّهُمْ ◄ اَبْوَابَ كُلِّ شَىْءٍ ◄
20

اِنْ اَجْرِىَ اِلَّا عَلٰى رَبِّ الْعٰلَمِيْنَ ◄ كَانُوْا يَعْمَلُوْنَ ◄
21

Allāh سبحانه وتعالى says,

"In whatever condition you are and whatever part of the Qurʾān you are reciting, whatever work you are doing, We witness you when you are engaged in it."

(Sūrah Yūnus 10:61)

17

LEVEL

17ª Lām of Allāh

So far, I can apply the rules of:

- Ta'awwudh and Basmalah
- Mīm *Mushaddadah* and Nūn *Mushaddadah*
- Qalqalah

♥ **Tafkhīm** (تَفْخِيْم) **means:**
to raise the back of the tongue towards the palate when pronouncing a letter, as if the back of the mouth is full.

♥ **The rule is:**
when "Lām of Allāh" is after a *fatḥah* or *ḍammah*, it will be full-mouth, and when it is after a *kasrah*, it will be empty-mouth.

♥ **For example:**

فِيْ دِيْنِ اللهِ ، هُوَ اللهُ

Tip:
You should only encircle your lips to pronounce Wāw (و) or any letter with *ḍammah*. It is a common mistake to encircle the lips to make a letter full-mouth; for example, صِرَاطَ.

Spot the rule

Every time I see this rule, I will say:
"Lām of Allāh, after *kasrah*: empty-mouth"
or "Lām of Allāh, after *fatḥah/ḍammah*: full-mouth".

NOTES

اَلْحَمْدُ لِلّٰهِ ◄ اٰمَنَّا بِاللّٰهِ ◄ بِاٰيٰتِ اللّٰهِ ◄ مِنَ اللّٰهِ

4 3 2 1

فَزَادَهُمُ اللّٰهُ ◄ اَللّٰهُ الصَّمَدُ ۟ ◄ وَاللّٰهُ مُحِيْطٌ ◄ وَاللّٰهُ

8 7 6 5

عَلِيْمٌ ◄ وَاللّٰهُ الْمُسْتَعَانُ ◄ عَهْدَ اللّٰهِ ◄ اَمْرُ اللّٰهِ

11 10 9

فَاَخَذَهُ اللّٰهُ ◄ كِتٰبَ اللّٰهِ ◄ صِبْغَةَ اللّٰهِ ◄ وَلْيَتَّقِ

15 14 13 12

اللّٰهَ ◄ وَاللّٰهُ يَهْدِىْ ◄ وَيُعَلِّمُكُمُ اللّٰهُ ◄ اَنَّ اللّٰهَ

18 17 16

يَعْلَمُ ◄ فَسَيَكْفِيْكَهُمُ اللّٰهُ ◄ قُلْ اٰمَنَّا بِاللّٰهِ

20 19

اَعُوْذُ بِاللّٰهِ ◄ يَسْمَعُوْنَ كَلٰمَ اللّٰهِ ◄ لَا تَعْبُدُوْنَ

23 22 21

اِلَّا اللّٰهَ ◄ مَنْ اٰمَنَ بِاللّٰهِ ◄ فَتْحُ اللّٰهِ عَلَيْكُمْ

25 24

اللّٰهُ يَسْتَهْزِئُ بِهِمْ ◄ فَتَبٰرَكَ اللّٰهُ ◄ كَمَا عَلَّمَهُ اللّٰهُ

28 27 26

وَمَا اللّٰهُ بِغَافِلٍ ◄ سَيَقُوْلُوْنَ لِلّٰهِ ◄ فِيْ سَبِيْلِ

31 30 29

اللّٰهِ ◄ اَنِ اعْبُدُوا اللّٰهَ ◄ يُبَشِّرُ اللّٰهُ عِبَادَهُ ◄ اِلَّا

34 33 32

بِاِذْنِ اللّٰهِ ◄ لَوْلَا يُكَلِّمُنَا اللّٰهُ ◄ تِلْكَ حُدُوْدُ اللّٰهِ

36 35

مَتٰى نَصْرُ اللّٰهِ ◄ وَاَحَلَّ اللّٰهُ الْبَيْعَ ◄ وَيَكُوْنَ

39 38 37

HOMEWORK KEY	TIME (MIN)	MON	TUE	WED	THU	FRI	SAT	SUN	PARENT INITIALS	PASS STAMP	START DATE
✓ DUE	WEEK 1										
✓ PASS	WEEK 2										PASS DATE

NOTES

الَّذِينَ لِلّٰهِ ◂ يَعِظُكُمُ اللّٰهُ ◂ حَتّٰى يُغْنِيَهُمُ ²

اللّٰهُ ◂ فَاَخَذَهُمُ اللّٰهُ بِذُنُوبِهِمْ ◂ يَغْفِرُ اللّٰهُ ⁴

لَكُمْ ◂ وَاللّٰهُ اللّٰهُ الْمَلِكَ ◂ يُدْعَوْنَ اِلٰى ⁶ ⁵

كِتٰبُ اللّٰهِ ◂ اَمْ تَقُولُونَ عَلَى اللّٰهِ ◂ يُوَفِّيهِمُ اللّٰهُ ⁸ ⁷

دِينَهُمْ ◂ كَذٰلِكَ يُحِي اللّٰهُ الْمَوْتٰى ◂ اَنَّ الْقُوَّةَ ¹⁰ ⁹

لِلّٰهِ جَمِيعًا ◂ عَلَى الَّذِينَ هَدَى اللّٰهُ ◂ فَاَمَاتَهُ ¹² ¹¹

اللّٰهُ مِائَةَ عَامٍ ◂ فَاِنَّ اللّٰهَ يَاْتِى بِالشَّمْسِ ◂ اِنَّ ¹⁴ ¹³

هُدَى اللّٰهِ هُوَ الْهُدٰى ◂ وَمَا مِنَ اللّٰهِ اِلَّا اللّٰهُ ¹⁵

فَاذْكُرُوا اللّٰهَ كَمَا عَلَّمَكُمْ ◂ وَاِذَا قِيلَ لَهُ اتَّقِ ¹⁷ ¹⁶

اللّٰهَ ◂ فَلَوْلَا فَضْلُ اللّٰهِ عَلَيْكُمْ ◂ وَيَضْرِبُ اللّٰهُ ¹⁹ ¹⁸

الْاَمْثَالَ لِلنَّاسِ ◂ فَتَعٰلَى اللّٰهُ الْمَلِكُ الْحَقُّ ²⁰

مِنْ اَحَدٍ اِلَّا بِاِذْنِ اللّٰهِ ◂ وَمَنْ اَحْسَنُ مِنَ اللّٰهِ ²² ²¹

صِبْغَةً ◂ اَيْنَ مَا تَكُونُوا يَاْتِ بِكُمُ اللّٰهُ جَمِيعًا ²³

NOTES

وَاللّٰهُ اَعْلَمُ بِمَا ◄ كَذٰلِكَ يُبَيِّنُ اللّٰهُ لَكُمُ الْاٰيٰتِ ◄

قُلْ اِنَّ ◄ يَهْدِى اللّٰهُ لِنُوْرِهٖ ◄ وَضَعَتْ ◄

وَيَقُوْلُوْنَ عَلَى اللّٰهِ الْكَذِبَ ◄ الْفَضْلَ بِيَدِ اللّٰهِ ◄

يَدْخُلُوْنَ فِيْ ◄ فَاِنَّهٗ نَزَّلَهٗ عَلٰى قَلْبِكَ بِاِذْنِ اللّٰهِ ◄

اَلَمْ تَعْلَمْ اَنَّ اللّٰهَ لَهٗ مُلْكُ ◄ دِيْنِ اللّٰهِ اَفْوَاجًا ۟

ذٰلِكَ ◄ بَلٰى مَنْ اَسْلَمَ وَجْهَهٗ لِلّٰهِ ◄ السَّمٰوٰتِ ◄

اِنَّمَا يَعْمُرُ مَسٰجِدَ ◄ بِاَنَّ اللّٰهَ نَزَّلَ الْكِتٰبَ بِالْحَقِّ ◄

قَالَ اِنَّ اللّٰهَ اصْطَفٰهُ ◄ اللّٰهِ مَنْ اٰمَنَ بِاللّٰهِ ◄

فَاللّٰهُ ◄ وَمَا كَانَ اللّٰهُ لِيُضِيْعَ اِيْمَانَكُمْ ◄ عَلَيْكُمْ ◄

اَيَّامَ ◄ لَا يَرْجُوْنَ ◄ يَحْكُمُ بَيْنَهُمْ يَوْمَ الْقِيٰمَةِ ◄

قَالَ ◄ فَقُلْ اَسْلَمْتُ وَجْهِيَ لِلّٰهِ وَمَنِ اتَّبَعَنِ ◄ اللّٰهِ ◄

وَلَا يُكَلِّمُهُمُ اللّٰهُ ◄ اَنّٰى يُحْيٖ هٰذِهِ اللّٰهُ بَعْدَ مَوْتِهَا ◄

اَنْ اٰتٰهُ اللّٰهُ الْمُلْكَ ◄ يَوْمَ الْقِيٰمَةِ وَلَا يُزَكِّيْهِمْ ◄

HOMEWORK KEY	TIME (MIN)	MON	TUE	WED	THU	FRI	SAT	SUN	PARENT INITIALS	PASS STAMP	START DATE
✓ DUE	WEEK 1									⭐	PASS DATE
✓ PASS	WEEK 2										

17b Rā Mutaḥarrikah (رَاءٌ مُتَحَرِّكَة)

So far, I can apply the rules of:

- *Ta'awwudh* and *Basmalah*
- Mīm *Mushaddadah* and Nūn *Mushaddadah*
- *Qalqalah*
- Lām of Allāh

The rule is:
When Rā has a *ḍammah* or *fatḥah*, it will be full-mouth, and when it has a *kasrah*, it will be empty-mouth.

For example:

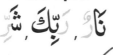

نَارٌ , رَبِّكَ , شَرِّ

Note:
"Rā *Mutaḥarrikah*" includes Rā with *fatḥatayn, ḍammatayn* or *kasratayn,* as well as Rā with *shaddah*; the Rā will be read according to its *ḥarakah*.

Spot the rule

Every time I see this rule, I will say:
"Rā with *kasrah*: empty-mouth"
or "Rā with *fatḥah/ḍammah*: full-mouth".

NOTES

فَاحْذَرُوهُ ۞ وَلَا شَرَابًا ۞ وَإِذَا رَأَوْهُمْ ۞ وَاشْكُرُوا

4   3   2   1

لِي ۞ هُوَ رَابِعُهُمْ ۞ رَسُولُ اللَّهِ ۞ رَبِّ السَّمَاوَاتِ ۞ وَرَأَوُا

8   7   6   5

الْعَذَابَ ۞ فَشَرِبُوا مِنْهُ ۞ وَبُرِّزَتِ الْجَحِيمُ ۞ فَأَكْرَمَهُ

11   10   9

وَنَعَّمَهُ ۞ وَالَّذِينَ كَفَرُوا ۞ إِنَّهَا تَذْكِرَةٌ ۞ رَفَعَ

14   13   12

سَمْكَهَا ۞ وَكُلُوا وَاشْرَبُوا ۞ وَنُيَسِّرُكَ لِلْيُسْرَىٰ

16   15

الْجَوَارِ الْكُنَّسِ ۞ شَهْرُ رَمَضَانَ ۞ إِلَىٰ صِرَاطٍ

19   18   17

فَالْمُدَبِّرَاتِ أَمْرًا ۞ تَتْبَعُهَا الرَّادِفَةُ ۞ لِنُخْرِجَ

22   21   20

بِهِ حَبًّا ۞ ذَاتِ الرَّجْعِ ۞ لَا تُلْهِيهِمْ تِجَارَةٌ ۞ مَا

25   24   23

غَرَّكَ بِرَبِّكَ ۞ فَاسْتَبِقُوا الْخَيْرَاتِ ۞ ثُمَّ السَّبِيلَ

27   26

يَسَّرَهُ ۞ يَوْمَ يَقُومُ الرُّوحُ ۞ وَإِذَا مَرُّوا بِهِمْ ۞ الْحَقُّ

30   29   28

مِن رَّبِّكَ ۞ فَهُوَ خَيْرٌ لَّهُ ۞ وَيَقُولُ الْكَافِرُ يَالَيْتَنِي

32   31

إِنَّ الَّذِينَ أَجْرَمُوا ۞ ثُمَّ أَدْبَرَ يَسْعَىٰ ۞ وَالْأَمْرُ يَوْمَئِذٍ

35   34   33

ثُمَّ أَمَاتَهُ فَأَقْبَرَهُ ۞ وَإِذَا الْقُبُورُ بُعْثِرَتْ ۞ وَأَثَرَ

38   37   36

Handwritten notes: roth raah · With · ghunnah · Lwaley · Make Sure · you go · slow · tell ur · b.ro or sis · to double · check

HOMEWORK KEY	TIME (MIN)	MON	TUE	WED	THU	FRI	SAT	SUN	PARENT INITIALS	PASS STAMP	START DATE
✓ DUE	WEEK 1										PASS DATE
✓ PASS	WEEK 2										

NOTES

إِذَا الشَّمْسُ ◀ وَإِذَا الْبِحَارُ فُجِّرَتْ ۥ ◀ الْحَيٰوةَ الدُّنْيَا ۥ ١

كَذٰلِكَ يُرِيهِمُ ◀ وَالَّذِيْ قَدَّرَ فَهَدٰى ۥ ◀ كُوِّرَتْ ۥ ٣ ٢

فَقَدَرَ عَلَيْهِ رِزْقَهٗ ۥ ٥ / آوْ نَرٰى رَبَّنَا ◀ اللّٰهُ ٦ ٤

وَإِذَا ◀ وَإِذَا الْوُحُوشُ حُشِرَتْ ۥ ◀ وَإِذَا الْبِحَارُ سُجِّرَتْ ۥ ٧ ٨

وَأُذِنَتْ ◀ وَإِذَا الْعِشَارُ عُطِّلَتْ ۥ ◀ الْجَحِيْمُ سُعِّرَتْ ۥ ٩ ١٠ ١١

وَإِذَا ◀ وَإِذَا الْجِبَالُ سُيِّرَتْ ۥ ◀ لِرَبِّهَا وَحُقَّتْ ۥ ١٢ ١٣

إِنَّ ◀ وَلَا تُمْسِكُوْهُنَّ ضِرَارًا ◀ الصُّحُفُ نُشِرَتْ ۥ ١٤ ١٥

سَبِّحِ اسْمَ ◀ وَهُوَ خَيْرُ النَّاصِرِيْنَ ◀ فِيْ ذٰلِكَ لَعِبْرَةً / ١٦ ١٧

اِذْ تَبَرَّأَ ◀ وَلَوْ يَرَى الَّذِيْنَ ظَلَمُوْا ◀ رَبِّكَ الْأَعْلَى ۥ ١٨ ١٩

الَّذِيْ ◀ فَمَنِ اضْطُرَّ غَيْرَ بَاغٍ / ◀ الَّذِيْنَ اتَّبَعُوْا ٢٠ ٢١

وَأَتِمُّوا الْحَجَّ وَالْعُمْرَةَ ◀ يَصْلَى النَّارَ الْكُبْرٰى ۥ ٢٢

إِذَا حَضَرَ ◀ فَأَلْهَمَهَا فُجُوْرَهَا وَتَقْوٰىهَا ۥ ◀ لِلّٰهِ ٢٣ ٢٤

الَمْ تَرَ إِلَى الَّذِيْنَ خَرَجُوْا ◀ أَحَدَكُمُ الْمَوْتُ ٢٥

START DATE
PASS DATE
PASS STAMP

	TIME (MIN)	MON	TUE	WED	THU	FRI	SAT	SUN	PARENT INITIALS
WEEK 1									
WEEK 2									

CORRECTION KEY

STRETCH LETTER
FLUENCY
JOIN
HARAKA
PRONUNCIATIC
يَسْعَى

NOTES

فَمَا اسْتَيْسَرَ مِنَ الْهَدْيِ ۚ بِالَّيْلِ وَ النَّهَارِ ١

سِرًّا ۞ قُلْ لِّلّٰهِ الْمَشْرِقُ وَالْمَغْرِبُ ۚ وَعَلَى ٣

الْوَارِثِ مِثْلُ ذٰلِكَ ۚ وَلَمَّا بَرَزُوا لِجَالُوتَ ٥

وَجُنُودِهٖ ۞ إِنَّمَا حَرَّمَ عَلَيْكُمُ الْمَيْتَةَ ۞ كَذٰلِكَ ٧

يُرِيهِمُ اللّٰهُ اَعْمَالَهُمْ ۞ فَإِنْ خَرَجْنَ فَلَا جُنَاحَ ٨

عَلَيْكُمْ ۞ وَاَمَّا مَنْ خَافَ مَقَامَ رَبِّهٖ ۞ وَسُيِّرَتِ ٩

الْجِبَالُ فَكَانَتْ سَرَابًا ۞ يَعْلَمُ الْجَهْرَ وَمَا يَخْفٰى ۞ ١١

وَلِتُكَبِّرُوا اللّٰهَ عَلٰى مَا هَدَاكُمْ ۞ فَمَهِّلِ الْكٰفِرِينَ ١٣

اَمْهِلْهُمْ رُوَيْدًا ۞ اِذْ نَادَاهُ رَبُّهٗ بِالْوَادِ الْمُقَدَّسِ ١٤

اِسْتَعِينُوا بِالصَّبْرِ وَالصَّلٰوةِ ۞ فَإِنْ خِفْتُمْ فَرِجَالًا ١٥

اَوْ رُكْبَانًا ۚ اِذْ تَبَرَّاَ الَّذِينَ اتُّبِعُوا مِنَ الَّذِينَ ١٧

اتَّبَعُوا ۞ عَلَى الْمُوسِعِ قَدَرُهٗ وَعَلَى الْمُقْتِرِ قَدَرُهٗ ۚ ١٨

وَعِبَادُ الرَّحْمٰنِ الَّذِينَ يَمْشُونَ عَلَى الْاَرْضِ هَوْنًا ١٩

When it
is stop

ت ـ ان ـ تـ تّ

17^c Rā Sākinah (رَاءٌ سَاكِنَة)

So far, I can apply the rules of:

- Ta'awwudh and Basmalah
- Mīm *Mushaddadah* and Nūn *Mushaddadah*
- Qalqalah
- Lām of Allāh
- Rā *Mutaḥarrikah*

♥ The rule is:

When Rā *Sākinah* is after a *fatḥah* or a *ḍammah*, it will be full-mouth, and when it is after a *kasrah*, it will be empty-mouth.

♥

For example:

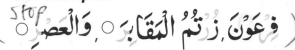

(فِرعَونَ , زُرْتُمُ الْمَقَابِرَ ○ , وَالْعَصْرِ ○)

Note:

"Rā *Sākinah*" refers to 2 things: (1) a Rā that is temporarily *sākin* because you stopped on that Rā, and (2) a Rā *Sākinah* that has another *sākin* letter before it.

Also, There are some exceptions to this rule which will be explained in the Advanced Tajwīd Book. For the time being, the teacher will inform the student of any exceptions in his Qur'ān homework.

Spot the rule

Every time I see this rule, I will say:

"Rā *Sākinah* after *kasrah*: empty-mouth"
or "Rā *Sākinah* after *fatḥah/ḍammah*: full-mouth".

وَالْفَجْرِ۟	اُذْكُرْكُمْ	فَبَشِّرْهُمْ	وَارْكَعُوا	فَذَكِّرْ
1	2	3	4	5
اسْتَكْبَرَتْ	وَاسْتَغْفِرْهُ	وَاغْفِرْلَنَا	وَمَرْعٰهَا	
6	7	8	9	
اَرْبَعِينَ	ثُمَّ اَقْرَرْتُمْ	فَلَا تَكْفُرْ	وَلَا بِكْرٌ	
10	11	12	13	
وَلَيَالٍ عَشْرٍ۟	اَيَّانَ مُرْسٰهَا	اٰلِ فِرْعَوْنَ	لَيْلَةً	
14	15	16		
قَالَ ءَاَقْرَرْتُمْ	اَلَا تَرْتَابُوا	وَقُضِيَ الْاَمْرُ		
17	18	19		
فَاِنْ اُحْصِرْتُمْ	وَالْيَوْمِ الْاٰخِرِ	بِيَدِكَ الْخَيْرُ		
20	21	22		
اَخْرَجَ الْمَرْعٰى	مَالَيْلَةُ الْقَدْرِ۟	اَلْهٰكُمُ التَّكَاثُرُ۟		
23	24	25		
فَصَرَهُنَّ	وَيُرْبِى الصَّدَقٰتِ	وَالشَّفْعِ وَالْوَتْرِ۟		
26	27	28		
اَعْطَيْنٰكَ الْكَوْثَرَ۟	حَتّٰى يَطْهُرْنَ	اِلَيْكَ		
29	30			
وَالْجِبَالَ	تَرْهَقُهَا قَتَرَةٌ	اَرْسَلْنٰكَ بِالْحَقِّ		
31	32	33		
اَرْسَلْنَا فِيكُمْ	وَتَوَاصَوْا بِالْمَرْحَمَةِ۟	اَرْسَلَهَا		
35	34			
حَتّٰى زُرْتُمُ الْمَقَابِرَ۟	وَاِلَيْهِ يُرْجَعُ الْاَمْرُ	رَسُولًا		
37	36			
فَاَحْيَا	ثُمَّ اِلٰى مَرْجِعِكُمْ	نَقْعًا۟	فَاَثَرْنَ بِهِ	
40	39	38		

NOTES

Because the letter before the ra sukin has a kasrah.

HOMEWORK KEY	TIME (MIN)	MON	TUE	WED	THU	FRI	SAT	SUN	PARENT INITIALS	PASS STAMP	START DATE
✔ DUE	WEEK 1									★	
✔ PASS	WEEK 2										PASS DATE

NOTES

مَطْلَعِ ◂ هِىَ حَتّٰى ◂ بَرْدًا لَّا يَذُوْقُوْنَ فِيْهَا ◂ بِهِ الْأَرْضَ ١

وَاِنِّىْ سَمَّيْتُهَا ◂ فَارْغَبْ ۝ وَاِلٰى رَبِّكَ ◂ الْفَجْرِ ٣

وَيَغْفِرْ لَكُمْ ◂ قُلْ هَاتُوْا بُرْهَانَكُمْ ◂ مَرْيَمَ ٥

يَوْمَ تَرْجُفُ ◂ فَبُهِتَ الَّذِىْ كَفَرَ ◂ ذُنُوْبَكُمْ ٧

اِضْرِبْ ◂ يُعَلِّمُوْنَ النَّاسَ السِّحْرَ ◂ الرَّاجِفَةُ ٩

لَا ◂ تَرَبُّصُ اَرْبَعَةِ اَشْهُرٍ ◂ بِّعَصَاكَ الْحَجَرُ ١١

وَانْحَرْ ◂ فَصَلِّ لِرَبِّكَ ◂ تُفْسِدُوْا فِى الْأَرْضِ ١٣

قُلْ اِصْلَاحٌ ◂ يُرْضِعْنَ اَوْلَادَهُنَّ ◂ وَالْوَالِدَاتُ ١٥

اِنَّ ◂ وَارْزُقْ اَهْلَهٗ مِنَ الثَّمَرٰتِ ◂ لَّهُمْ خَيْرٌ ١٧

وَلَا تَعْثَوْا فِى الْأَرْضِ ◂ شَانِئَكَ هُوَ الْأَبْتَرُ ۝ ١٨

يَسْـَٔلُوْنَكَ عَنِ الْخَمْرِ ◂ ءَاِنَّا لَمَرْدُوْدُوْنَ فِى الْحَافِرَةِ ١٩

وَاٰتَيْنَا ◂ وَيَوْمَ يُرْجَعُوْنَ اِلَيْهِ ◂ وَالْمَيْسِرِ ٢١

قُرِئَ عَلَيْهِمُ الْقُرْاٰنَ ◂ عِيْسَى ابْنَ مَرْيَمَ الْبَيِّنٰتِ ٢٣

START DATE
PASS DATE

PASS STAMP

TIME (MIN)	MON	TUE	WED	THU	FRI	SAT	SUN
WEEK 1							
WEEK 2							

PARENT INITIALS

CORRECTION KEY

STRETCH LETTER ········ HARAKA

JOIN ا

يَسْعٰى

FLUENCY ········ PRONUNCIATIC

NOTES

وَاغْفِرْلَنَا وَارْحَمْنَا ◄ وَاِذْ قُلْنَا ادْخُلُوا هٰذِهِ
1

الْقَرْيَةَ ◄ فَقَدِ اسْتَمْسَكَ بِالْعُرْوَةِ الْوُثْقٰى ◄ هُوَ
2   4

اَدْنٰى بِالَّذِىْ هُوَ خَيْرٌ ◄ يَوْمَ يَفِرُّ الْمَرْءُ مِنْ اَخِيْهِ ◌
5

وَذِى الْقُرْبٰى وَالْيَتٰمٰى وَالْمَسٰكِيْنِ ◄ الَّذِىْ لَهُ مُلْكُ
6   7

السَّمٰوٰتِ وَالْاَرْضِ ◌ اِنَّهُمْ كَانُوْا لَا يَرْجُوْنَ حِسَابًا ◌
8

هَلْ فِىْ ذٰلِكَ قَسَمٌ لِّذِىْ حِجْرٍ ◌ مَا يُفَرِّقُوْنَ بِهٖ
9   10

بَيْنَ الْمَرْءِ وَزَوْجِهٖ ◄ لَهُ مَا فِى السَّمٰوٰتِ وَمَا
11

فِى الْاَرْضِ ◄ هُوَ الَّذِىْ يُصَوِّرُكُمْ فِى الْاَرْحَامِ
12

اُمِرْتُ اَنْ اَعْبُدَ رَبَّ هٰذِهِ الْبَلْدَةِ ◄ وَاِذْ اٰتَيْنَا
13   14

مُوْسَى الْكِتٰبَ وَالْفُرْقَانَ ◄ وَاذْكُرْنَ مَا يُتْلٰى
15

فِىْ بُيُوْتِكُنَّ ◄ اَللّٰهُ الَّذِىْ يُرْسِلُ الرِّيٰحَ فَتُثِيْرُ
16

سَحَابًا ◄ وَاُولُوا الْاَرْحَامِ بَعْضُهُمْ اَوْلٰى بِبَعْضٍ
17

رَبِّ اِنِّىْ نَذَرْتُ لَكَ مَا فِىْ بَطْنِىْ مُحَرَّرًا
18

HOMEWORK KEY	TIME (MIN)	MON	TUE	WED	THU	FRI	SAT	SUN	PARENT INITIALS	PASS STAMP	START DATE
✔ DUE	WEEK 1 ►										PASS DATE
✔ PASS	WEEK 2 ►										

17d Full-mouth letters

So far, I can apply the rules of:

- ◯ *Ta'awwudh* and *Basmalah*
- ◯ Mīm *Mushaddadah* and Nūn *Mushaddadah*
- ◉ *Qalqalah*
- ◉ *Lām* of Allāh
- ◉ Rā *Mutaḥarrikah*
- ◯ Rā *Sākinah*

(♥) **The rule is:**

that the seven letters of خُصَّ ضَغَطٍ قِظْ (خ ص ض غ ط ق ظ) will always be read full-mouth.

(♥) **For example:**

خَلَقَ , سَيَصْلَى

Note:

Often, the letter before will be an empty-mouth letter. It is a common mistake to make the letter full as well when it should be empty; for example, the ىَ in سَيَصْلَى should be empty-mouth.

Spot the rule

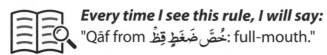

Every time I see this rule, I will say:

"Qāf from خُصَّ ضَغَطٍ قِظْ: full-mouth."

NOTES

وَالضُّحٰى ۝ ٤	وَالصَّيْفِ ۚ ٣	بِالْمَغْفِرَةِ ٢	وَصَاحِبَتِهٖ ١
وَلَا تَقُوْلُوْا ٨	تَرْضٰىهَا ٧	اِذَا يَغْشٰىهَا ٦	لِيُضِيْعَ ٥
اِيْمَانَكُمْ ١١	عَلٰى عَقِبَيْهِ ١٠	مَرْضَاتِ اللّٰهِ ٩	مِنْ
اَيَّامٍ اُخَرَ ۚ	عَلَيْهِمْ صَلَوٰتٌ ١٢	طَعَامُ مِسْكِيْنٍ ۚ ١٣	
وَبِالْاٰخِرَةِ ١٧	اَلَّتِيْ تَطَّلِعُ ١٦	كَلَّا لَا تُطِعْهُ ١٥	فَكَذَّبَ ١٤
وَعَصٰى ۚ	لِاِيْلٰفِ قُرَيْشٍ ۚ ۝ ١٩	فَاَحْيَا بِهِ الْاَرْضَ ١٨	
ذٰلِكَ الْيَوْمُ الْحَقُّ ۚ ٢٠	اِنَّ يَوْمَ الْفَصْلِ ٢١	اَظْلَمُ عَلَيْهِمْ ٢٢	
خٰلِدِيْنَ فِيْهَا ۚ ٢٣	اِشْتَرَوُا الضَّلٰلَةَ ٢٤	مِنَ الْغَمَامِ ٢٥	
وَاَقَامَ الصَّلٰوةَ ٢٦	اَلْوَصِيَّةُ لِلْوَالِدَيْنِ ٢٧	وَقُضِيَ ٢٨	
الْاَمْرُ ۚ	لَيَكْتُمُوْنَ الْحَقَّ ٢٩	كُتِبَ عَلَيْكُمُ الصِّيَامُ ٣٠	
وَبَنَيْنَا فَوْقَكُمْ ٣١	وَصَدَّقَ بِالْحُسْنٰى ۝ ٣٢	كَذَّبَتْ ثَمُوْدُ ٣٣	
بِطَغْوٰىهَا ۝	لِسَعْيِهَا رَاضِيَةٌ ۚ ۝ ٣٤	وَالَّيْلِ اِذَا يَغْشٰى ٣٥	
وَاَخْرَجَتِ الْاَرْضُ ٣٦	لَا يُصِيْبُهُمْ ظَمَأٌ ٣٧	وَنَمَارِقُ ٣٨	

HOMEWORK KEY	TIME (MIN)	MON	TUE	WED	THU	FRI	SAT	SUN	PARENT INITIALS	PASS STAMP	START DATE
✓ DUE	WEEK 1										PASS DATE
✓ PASS	WEEK 2										

NOTES

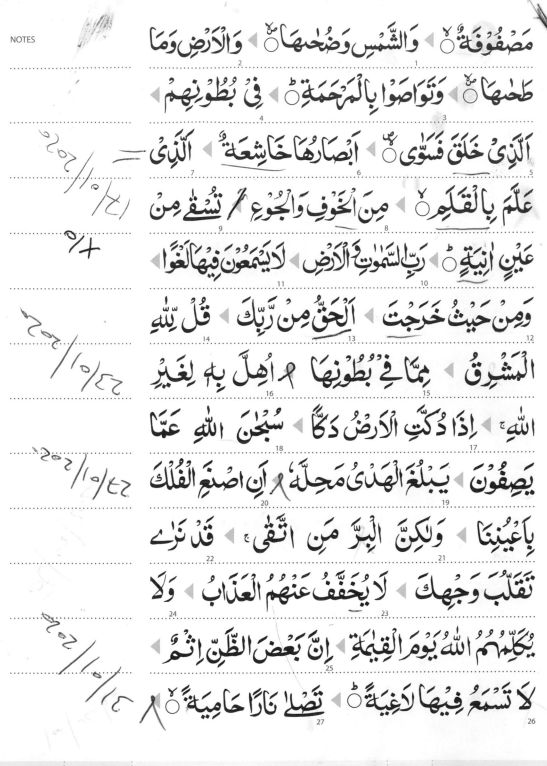

وَالشَّمْسِ وَضُحٰىهَا ◀ مَصْفُوفَةٌ

وَالْأَرْضِ وَمَا ◀ 1

فِى بُطُونِهِمْ ◀ وَتَوَاصَوْا بِالْمَرْحَمَةِ ◀ 3

طَحٰىهَا ◀ 4

اَلَّذِى ◀ أَبْصَارُهَا خَاشِعَةٌ ◀ اَلَّذِى خَلَقَ فَسَوّٰى ◀ 5

7

6

تُسْقٰى مِنْ ◀ مِنَ الْخَوْفِ وَالْجُوْعِ ◀ عَلَّمَ بِالْقَلَمِ ◀ 8

9

لَا يَسْمَعُونَ فِيهَا لَغْوًا ◀ رَبِّ السَّمٰوٰتِ وَالْأَرْضِ ◀ عَيْنٍ اٰنِيَةٍ ◀ 10

11

قُلْ لِلّٰهِ ◀ اَلْحَقُّ مِنْ رَبِّكَ ◀ وَمِنْ حَيْثُ خَرَجْتَ ◀ 12

13

14

أُهِلَّ بِهٖ لِغَيْرِ ◀ مِمَّا فِى بُطُونِهَا ◀ الْمَشْرِقُ ◀ 16

15

سُبْحٰنَ اللّٰهِ عَمَّا ◀ إِذَا دُكَّتِ الْأَرْضُ دَكًّا ◀ اللّٰهِ ◀ 17

18

أَنْ اصْنَعِ الْفُلْكَ ◀ يَبْلُغَ الْهَدْىُ مَحِلَّهُ ◀ يَصِفُونَ ◀ 19

20

قَدْ نَرٰى ◀ وَلٰكِنَّ الْبِرَّ مَنِ اتَّقٰى، ◀ بِأَعْيُنِنَا ◀ 21

22

وَلَا ◀ لَا يُخَفَّفُ عَنْهُمُ الْعَذَابُ ◀ تَقَلُّبَ وَجْهِكَ ◀ 23

24

إِنَّ بَعْضَ الظَّنِّ إِثْمٌ ◀ يُكَلِّمُهُمُ اللّٰهُ يَوْمَ الْقِيٰمَةِ ◀ 25

تَصْلٰى نَارًا حَامِيَةً ◀ لَا تَسْمَعُ فِيهَا لَاغِيَةً ◀ 26

27

START DATE

PASS DATE

PASS STAMP

TIME (MIN) | MON | TUE | WED | THU | FRI | SAT | SUN

WEEK 1

WEEK 2

PARENT INITIALS

CORRECTION KEY

JOIN
HARAK
STRETCH
LETTER
يَسْمَعِ
FLUENCY
PRONUNCIATI

NOTES

لَا تُفْسِدُوا وَفِى الْاَرْضِ ◄ وَالْقَتْ مَا فِيهَا وَتَخَلَّتْ ۞ ۱

غَيْرِ الْمَغْضُوبِ عَلَيْهِمْ ◄ وَالْاَرْضَ بَعْدَ ذٰلِكَ ۳

دَحٰهَا ۞ وَاَغْطَشَ لَيْلَهَا وَاَخْرَجَ ضُحٰهَا ۞ مِنْ اَيِّ ۵

شَىْءٍ خَلَقَهُ ۞ اَلَّذِى خَلَقَكَ فَسَوّٰىكَ فَعَدَلَكَ ۷

قُلْ هِىَ مَوَاقِيتُ لِلنَّاسِ ◄ وَابْتَغُوا مَا كَتَبَ اللهُ ۹

لَكُمْ ص نَزَّلَ الْفُرْقَانَ عَلٰى عَبْدِهٖ وَيَشْهَدُ ۱۰

اللهُ عَلٰى مَا فِى قَلْبِهٖ ◄ وَخَلَقَ كُلَّ شَىْءٍ اِلَّا ۱۲

اَلَّذِينَ ظَلَمُوا مِنْهُمْ ◄ مِنْ حَيْثُ اَفَاضَ ۱۴

النَّاسُ ◄ وَكُلَّ شَىْءٍ اَحْصَيْنٰهُ كِتٰبًا ۞ وَلَقَدْ ۱۵

صَرَّفْنٰهُ بَيْنَهُمْ لِيَذَّكَّرُوا اَلَّذِينَ اٰمَنُوا وَعَمِلُوا ۱۷

الصّٰلِحٰتِ ◄ اَمْلَيْتُ لَهَا وَهِىَ ظَالِمَةٌ ◄ وَثَمُودَ ۱۸

اَلَّذِينَ جَابُوا الصَّخْرَ ◄ اَلَمْ تَرَ اِلٰى رَبِّكَ كَيْفَ مَدَّ ۲۰

الظِّلَّ ◄ اُذِنَ لِلَّذِينَ يُقْتَلُونَ بِاَنَّهُمْ ظُلِمُوا ۲۱

17ᵉ Alif

So far, I can apply the rules of:

- Taʿawwudh and Basmalah
- Mīm *Mushaddadah* and Nūn *Mushaddadah*
- Qalqalah
- Lām of Allāh
- Rā *Mutaḥarrikah*
- Rā *Sākinah*

♥ **The rule is:**

If Alif follows a full-mouth letter, it will be full-mouth, and if it follows an empty-mouth letter, it will be empty-mouth.

♥ **For example:**

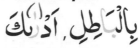

Note:

"Full-mouth letters" in this rule includes Rā and "Lām of Allāh" when they are full-mouth, as well as the letters of خُصَّ ضَغَطٍ قِظْ.

Spot the rule

Every time I see this rule, I will say:
"Alif after full-mouth letter: full-mouth"
or "Alif after empty-mouth letter: empty-mouth".

NOTES

١ يَخْطَفُ اَبْصَارَهُمْ ٢ يُخَادِعُونَ اللّٰهَ ٣ اٰمَنَ النَّاسُ

٤ تَشَابَهَتْ قُلُوبُهُمْ ٥ لَا تَقُولُوا رَاعِنَا ٦ وَوَصّٰى بِهَا

٧ وَسَعٰى فِي ٨ مَا لَوْنُهَا ٩ مَا الْقَارِعَةُ ١٠ اَلْقَارِعَةُ

١١ وَجَعَلْنَا نَوْمَكُمْ سُبَاتًا ١٢ وَعَمِلَ صَالِحًا ١٣ خَرَابِهَا

١٣ فَاَذْرَاَتُمْ فِيهَا ١٤ وَالنّٰزِعٰتِ غَرْقًا ١٥ فِيهَا سِرَاجًا

١٦ وَاَقَامَ الصَّلٰوةَ ١٧ لِمَنِ اتَّقٰى ١٨ خٰلِدِينَ فِيهَا

١٩ وَاِذَا خَاطَبَهُمْ ٢٠ اُوتُوا الْكِتٰبَ ٢١ اَلَّذِينَ تَابُوا

٢٢ اِنِ اسْتَطَاعُوا ٢٣ فَتَابَ عَلَيْكُمْ ٢٤ مَا وَلَّهُمْ

٢٥ وَالنّٰشِطٰتِ نَشْطًا ٢٦ وَالسّٰبِحٰتِ سَبْحًا ٢٧ وَالْجِبَالَ

٢٨ نَغْفِرْ لَكُمْ خَطٰيٰكُمْ ٢٩ لِلطّٰاغِينَ مَاٰبًا ٢٩ اَوْتَادًا

٣٠ وَلَا تَشْتَرُوا ٣١ فَالسّٰبِقٰتِ سَبْقًا ٣٢ وَعَمِلُوا الصّٰلِحٰتِ

٣٣ فَاَخَذَتْكُمُ الصّٰعِقَةُ ٣٤ قَالُوا سَلٰمًا ٣٥ ذٰلِكَ بِاٰيٰتِي

٣٦ قِيلَ لَهُمْ اٰمَنُوا ٣٧ اَلْكِتٰبُ لَا رَيْبَ وَاِذْ قَالَ

NOTES

مُوسٰى ◀ وَلَا يُقْبَلُ مِنْهَا شَفَاعَةٌ ◀ قَالُوا سُبْحٰنَكَ ١

لَا عِلْمَ لَنَا ◀ وَظَلَّلْنَا عَلَيْكُمُ الْغَمَامَ ◀ قُلْ هَاتُوا ٣

بُرْهَانَكُمْ ◀ لَا يُخَفَّفُ عَنْهُمْ / فَأَلْقٰى عَصَاهُ ◀ اِنَّ ٥

لَنَا لَأَجْرًا ◀ وَفِي الْاٰخِرَةِ حَسَنَةً ◀ مِنْ اٰيَامٍ ٨

أُخَرَ ◀ اٰمَنَّا بِرَبِّ الْعٰلَمِينَ ۝ ◀ وَلَا جِدَالَ ١٠

فِي الْحَجِّ ◀ فِي الدُّنْيَا وَالْاٰخِرَةِ ◀ وَالْجِفْنٰى ١٢

بِالصّٰلِحِينَ ◀ شَرِّ غَاسِقٍ اِذَا وَقَبَ ◀ اَنَّ الْقُوَّةَ ١٤

لِلّٰهِ جَمِيعًا ◀ وَاِنْ عَزَمُوا الطَّلَاقَ ◀ فَأَحْيَا بِهِ ١٦

الْاَرْضَ ◀ فَمَنِ اضْطُرَّ غَيْرَ بَاغٍ ◀ وَاِذْ نَادٰى ١٨

رَبُّكَ مُوسٰى ◀ اِنَّ فِي ذٰلِكَ لَاٰيَةً | وَقَالُوا ٢٠

قُلُوبُنَا غُلْفٌ ◀ تَظْهَرُونَ عَلَيْهِمْ ◀ حَتّٰى زُرْتُمُ ٢٢

الْمَقَابِرَ ◀ وَاِذْ اَخَذْنَا مِيثَاقَكُمْ ◀ وَادْخُلُوا الْبَابَ ٢٤

سُجَّدًا ◀ يَتْلُونَهُ حَقَّ تِلَاوَتِهِ ◀ وَمَا عَلَيْكَ اَلَّا ٢٦

START DATE		PASS STAMP	TIME (MIN)	MON	TUE	WED	THU	FRI	SAT	SUN	PARENT INITIALS
PASS DATE		★	WEEK 1								
			WEEK 2								

CORRECTION KEY

JOIN
STRETCH HARAK
LETTER يَسْعٰى
FLUENCY
PRONUNCIATI

NOTES

وَفُوۡمِهَا وَعَدَسِهَا ۗ ۝ وَمَنۡ خَفَّتۡ مَوَازِيۡنُهٗ ۝ يُزَكِّيۡ ۗ

يَقُوۡلُ ◄ وَاِذَا خَلَا بَعۡضُهُمۡ اِلٰى بَعۡضٍ ◄ وَبَصَلِهَا ۗ

حَيۡثُ ◄ وَكُلَا مِنۡهَا رَغَدًا ◄ يٰلَيۡتَنِىۡ قَدَّمۡتُ لِحَيَاتِىۡ ۝

اِذَا زُلۡزِلَتِ ◄ قُلۡنَا اهۡبِطُوۡا مِنۡهَا جَمِيۡعًا ◄ شِئۡتُمَا ۗ

فِى الدُّنۡيَا ◄ وَلَقَدِ اصۡطَفَيۡنٰهُ ۝ الۡاَرۡضُ زِلۡزَالَهَا ۝

حَدِيۡثُ ◄ هَلۡ اَتٰىكَ ◄ اُجِيۡبُ دَعۡوَةَ الدَّاعِ اِذَا دَعَانِ ۗ

اِذَا سَاَلَكَ ◄ هَلۡ اَتٰىكَ حَدِيۡثُ مُوۡسٰى ◄ الۡغَاشِيَةِ ۗ

خٰضِعِيۡنَ ◄ فَظَلَّتۡ اَعۡنَاقُهُمۡ لَهَا ◄ عِبَادِىۡ عَنِّىۡ ۗ

اَقِيۡمُوا الصَّلٰوةَ ◄ قَالَ اِنِّىۡ جَاعِلُكَ لِلنَّاسِ اِمَامًا

وَالۡحَجِّ ۗ ◄ هِىَ مَوَاقِيۡتُ لِلنَّاسِ ◄ وَاٰتُوا الزَّكٰوةَ

وَقَالُوۡا كُوۡنُوۡا ◄ فَجَعَلۡنٰهَا نَكَالًا لِّمَا بَيۡنَ يَدَيۡهَا ◄

وَمَا يَعۡلَمُ مِنۡ اَحَدٍ ◄ هُوۡدًا اَوۡ نَصٰرٰى تَهۡتَدُوۡا ۗ

اَلَّذِيۡنَ هَادُوۡا وَالنَّصٰرٰى وَالصّٰبِئِيۡنَ ◄ حَتّٰى يَقُوۡلَا ◄

HOMEWORK KEY	TIME (MIN)	MON	TUE	WED	THU	FRI	SAT	SUN	PARENT INITIALS	PASS STAMP	START DATE
✓ DUE	WEEK 1										
✓ PASS	WEEK 2										PASS DATE

The Prophet ﷺ said that

there is no envy (allowed) except regarding two individuals: a man whom Allāh has taught the Qur'ān and, as a result, he recites it throughout the night and day, and a man to whom Allāh ﷾ has given wealth and, as a result, he spends it all for the truth.

(Bukhārī: 5026)

18
LEVEL

18 a Ikhfā' Shafawī (إِخْفَاءشَفَوِي)

So far, I can apply the rules of:

- ✓ *Ta'awwudh* and *Basmalah*
- ✓ Mīm *Mushaddadah* and Nūn *Mushaddadah*
- ✓ *Qalqalah*
- ✓ *Tafkhīm*

♥ **Ikhfā' Shafawī means:**
for the lips to touch lightly during the *ghunnah*. At the end of the *ghunnah*, the lips will be pressed firmly together to pronounce the Bā.

♥ **The rule is:**
if Mīm *Sākinah* appears before Bā, there will be Ikhfā' Shafawī with *ghunnah*.

♥ **For example:**

يُحَاسِبْكُمْ بِهِ ، رَبَّهُمْ بِهِمْ

Spot the rule

Every time I see this rule, I will say:
"Mīm *Sākinah* before Bā: Ikhfā' Shafawī with *ghunnah*."

NOTES

يَعْتَصِم بِاللهِ ◄ اَيَاۡمُرُكُم بِالْكُفْرِ ◄ يَعِظُكُم بِهٖ ◄

تَعْرِفُهُم بِسِيْمٰهُمْ ◄ وَلَسْتُم بِاٰخِذِيْهِ ◄ وَلَنَبْلُوَنَّكُم

بِشَيْءٍ ◄ وَمَا هُم بِخٰرِجِيْنَ / وَمَا بَعْضُهُم بِتَابِعٍ ◄

يُحَاسِبْكُم بِهِ اللهُ ◄ فَاِذَا هُم بِالسَّاهِرَةِ ۚ ◌ اَلَمْ

يَعْلَمۡ بِاَنَّ اللهَ يَرٰى ۚ ◌ فَاَصْبَحْتُم بِنِعْمَتِهٖ ◄ لَيْسَ

لَكُم بِهٖ عِلْمٌ ◄ فَلِمَ يُعَذِّبُكُم بِذُنُوْبِكُمْ ◄ مَا لَهُم

بِهٖ مِنْ عِلْمٍ ◄ وَهُم بِالْاٰخِرَةِ / وَمَا لَيْسَ لَهُمْ

بِهٖ عِلْمٌ ◄ فِيْمَا تَرَاضَيْتُم بِهٖ ◄ وَاِذَا حُيِّيْتُم

بِتَحِيَّةٍ / لَا قِبَلَ لَهُم بِهَا ◄ فَهَزَمُوهُم بِاِذْنِ

اللهِ ◄ يَلْوٗنَ اَلْسِنَتَهُم بِالْكِتٰبِ ◄ مَا لَهُم بِذٰلِكَ

مِنْ عِلْمٍ / اَنّٖ قَدْ جِئْتُكُم بِاٰيَةٍ ◄ يَرُدُّوْكُم

بَعْدَ اِيْمَانِكُمْ ◄ فَاَتْبَعْنَا بَعْضَهُم بَعْضًا ◄ وَاللهُ

اَرْكَسَهُم بِمَا كَسَبُوۡا ◄ وَلِتَطْمَئِنَّ قُلُوْبُكُم بِهٖ ◄

NOTES

ذٰلِكُمْ وَصّٰكُمْ بِهٖ ◂ يَعْرِفُوْنَهُمْ بِسِيْمٰهُمْ ◂ اِذْ ۱

جِئْتُهُمْ بِالْبَيِّنٰتِ ◂ ذٰلِكَ جَزٰىهُمْ بِبَغْيِهِمْ ۚ ◂ وَلَقَدْ ۲

جِئْنٰهُمْ بِكِتٰبٍ ◂ فَاَهْلَكْنٰهُمْ بِذُنُوْبِهِمْ ◂ فَلَنُقَصِّصَنَّ ۳

عَلَيْهِمْ بِعِلْمٍ ◂ وَكَذٰلِكَ فَتَنَّا بَعْضَهُمْ بِبَعْضٍ ◂ ۴

وَاِذَا حَكَمْتُمْ بَيْنَ النَّاسِ ◂ تَظْهَرُوْنَ عَلَيْهِمْ ۵

بِالْاِثْمِ ◂ قَالَ قَدْ جِئْتُكُمْ بِالْحِكْمَةِ ◂ يُصِيْبَهُمْ ۶

بِبَعْضِ ذُنُوْبِهِمْ ◂ فَاِنْ اٰمَنَ بَعْضُكُمْ بَعْضًا ◂ وَاِذَا ۷

لَمْ تَاْتِهِمْ بِاٰيَةٍ ◂ لَا تُبْطِلُوْا صَدَقٰتِكُمْ بِالْمَنِّ ۸

وَالْاَذٰى ◂ يُمْدِدْكُمْ رَبُّكُمْ بِخَمْسَةِ اٰلٰفٍ ◂ وَمِيْثَاقَهُ ۹

الَّذِىْ وَاثَقَكُمْ بِهٖ ◂ فَيُنَبِّئُهُمْ بِمَا عَمِلُوْا ◂ وَهُمْ ۱۰

بَدَءُوْكُمْ اَوَّلَ مَرَّةٍ ◂ وَاَنِّيْ مُرْسِلَةٌ اِلَيْهِمْ ۱۱

بِهَدِيَّةٍ ◂ وَالَّذِيْنَ هُمْ بِرَبِّهِمْ لَا يُشْرِكُوْنَ ○ ◂ ۱۲

قَالَ اِنَّ اللهَ مُبْتَلِيْكُمْ بِنَهَرٍ ۚ ◂ اٰمَنَ ۱۳

NOTES

مِنْهُمْ بِاللّٰهِ وَالْيَوْمِ الْاٰخِرِ ◄ ذٰلِكَ قَوْلُهُمْ

بِأَفْوَاهِهِمْ ۚ ◄ وَلَا جُنَاحَ عَلَيْكُمْ فِيمَا عَرَّضْتُمْ

بِهٖ ◄ يُؤَاخِذُكُمْ بِمَا كَسَبَتْ قُلُوبُكُمْ ◄ وَاِنْ

حَكَمْتَ فَاحْكُمْ بَيْنَهُمْ بِالْقِسْطِ ◄ وَلَوْلَا دَفْعُ

اللّٰهِ النَّاسَ بَعْضَهُمْ بِبَعْضٍ ◄ يَدْعُوْنَ

رَبَّهُمْ بِالْغَدٰوةِ وَالْعَشِيِّ ◄ وَيُذِيْقَ بَعْضَكُمْ

بَأْسَ بَعْضٍ ◄ وَالَّذِيْنَ هُمْ بِاٰيٰتِ رَبِّهِمْ يُؤْمِنُوْنَ

يَعْلَمُ مَا جَرَحْتُمْ بِالنَّهَارِ ◄ وَلَا تَخَافُوْنَ اَنَّكُمْ

اَشْرَكْتُمْ بِاللّٰهِ ◄ وَهُوَ الَّذِيْ يَتَوَفّٰىكُمْ بِالَّيْلِ ◄

اَتُحَدِّثُوْنَهُمْ بِمَا فَتَحَ اللّٰهُ عَلَيْكُمْ ◄ وَلِاُحِلَّ لَكُمْ

بَعْضَ الَّذِيْ حُرِّمَ عَلَيْكُمْ ◄ فَاِذَا ذَهَبَ الْخَوْفُ

سَلَقُوْكُمْ بِاَلْسِنَةٍ ◄ قَدْ كَفَرْتُمْ بَعْدَ اِيْمَانِكُمْ ۚ

كُلَّمَا نَضِجَتْ جُلُوْدُهُمْ بَدَّلْنٰهُمْ جُلُوْدًا غَيْرَهَا ◄

18 b Idghām Shafawī (إِدْغَام شَفَوِي)

So far, I can apply the rules of:

✓ Ta'awwudh and Basmalah

✓ Mīm *Mushaddadah* and Nūn *Mushaddadah*

✓ Qalqalah

✓ Lām of Allāh

✓ Tafkhīm

✓ Ikhfā' Shafawī

♥ *Idghām Shafawī means:*
to merge two *mīms*.

♥ *The rule is:*
if Mīm *Sākinah* appears before another *mīm*, there will be *Idghām Shafawī* with *ghunnah*.

♥ *For example:*

وَءَامَنَهُم مِّن ، عَلَيْهِم مُّؤْصَدَةٌ

Note:
From here onwards, in examples like "وَعَلَيْكُمْ مَّا حُبِّلْتُمْ" the first Mīm *Mushaddadah* (وَعَلَيْكُمْ مَّا) should be identified as "*Idghām Shafawī* with *ghunnah*" and the second one (حُبِّلْتُمْ) should be identified as " Mīm *Mushaddadah, ghunnah*".

Spot the rule

Every time I see this rule, I will say:
"Mīm *Sākinah* before *mīm*: Idghām Shafawī with *ghunnah*."

NOTES

أَنَّكُم مُّلَاقُوهُ ◄ وَبَيْنَهُم مِّيثَاقٌ ◄ وَلَكُم مَّا كَسَبْتُمْ ◄

3 · · · · · · · · 2 · · · · · · · · 1

فَارْزُقُوهُم مِّنْهُ ◄ لَهُم مَّغْفِرَةٌ ◄ فِى قُلُوبِهِم

4 · · · · · · · · 5 · · · · · · · · 6

مَّرَضٌ ◄ فَمِنْهُم مَّنْ آمَنَ ◄ أَصَابَتْهُم مُّصِيبَةٌ ◄

7 · · · · · · · · 8

وَعَلَيْكُم مَّا حُمِّلْتُمْ ◄ أَنَّهُم مُّلَاقُوا اللّٰهِ ◄ وَأَمَنَهُم

11 · · · · · · · · 10 · · · · · · · · 9

مِّنْ خَوْفٍ ○ فَإِن لَّكُم مَّا سَأَلْتُمْ ◄ إِنَّهَا عَلَيْهِم

13 · · · · · · · · 12

مُّؤْصَدَةٌ ○ ◄ وَاللّٰهُ يَعِدُكُم مَّغْفِرَةً ◄ يُخْرِجُهُم

15 · · · · · · · · 14

مِّنَ الظُّلُمَاتِ ◄ وَآتَيْنَاهُم مُّلْكًا عَظِيمًا ○ ◄ وَأَخَوَاتُكُم

17 · · · · · · · · 16

مِّنَ الرَّضَاعَةِ ◄ فَبِمَا نَقْضِهِم مِّيثَاقَهُم ◄ مِن

19 · · · · · · · · 18

أَحَدِهِم مِّلْءُ الْأَرْضِ ◄ أَكْثَرُهُم بِهِم مُّؤْمِنُونَ ◄

20

وَأَمْطَرْنَا عَلَيْهِم مَّطَرًا ◄ وَرَزَقَكُم مِّنَ الطَّيِّبَاتِ ◄

21 · · · · · · · · 22

فَأَصَابَتْكُم مُّصِيبَةُ الْمَوْتِ ﻻ ◄ يُمَتِّعْكُم مَّتَاعًا

23 · · · · · · · · 24

حَسَنًا ◄ وَالَّذِينَ فِى قُلُوبِهِم مَّرَضٌ ◄ مَّا لَكُم

26 · · · · · · · · 25

مِّنَ اللّٰهِ غَيْرُهُ ﻻ ◄ يَغْفِرْ لَهُم مَّا قَدْ سَلَفَ ج ◄

27

HOMEWORK KEY	TIME (MIN)	MON	TUE	WED	THU	FRI	SAT	SUN	PARENT INITIALS	PASS STAMP	START DATE
✓ DUE	WEEK 1 ▸										PASS DATE
✓ PASS	WEEK 2 ▸										

NOTES

فَإِذَا قَضَيْتُم مَّنَاسِكَكُمْ ◀ وَيُجِرْكُم مِّنْ عَذَابٍ ◀
2 ... 1

وَمَا عَلَّمْتُم مِّنَ الْجَوَارِحِ ◀ وَعُلِّمْتُم مَّا لَمْ تَعْلَمُوا ◀
4 ... 3

فَشَرِّدْ بِهِم مَّنْ خَلْفَهُمْ ◀ أَخْرَجَ أَبَوَيْكُم مِّنَ
6 ... 5

الْجَنَّةِ ◀ هَلْ يَرَىٰكُم مِّنْ أَحَدٍ ◀ فَمَا سَأَلْتُكُم مِّنْ
8 ... 7

أَجْرٍ ط يُخْرِجُونَهُم مِّنَ النُّورِ ◀ فَإِنِ انْسَتُمْ
10 ... 9

مِّنْهُمْ رُشْدًا ◀ وَمِمَّنْ حَوْلَكُم مِّنَ الْأَعْرَابِ ◀ وَيَحْسَبُونَ
12 ... 11

أَنَّهُم مُّهْتَدُونَ ◀ اِتِيكُم مِّنْهَا بِخَبَرٍ ◀ أَخْرَجُوهُم
14 ... 13

مِّنْ حَيْثُ أَخْرَجُوكُمْ ◀ يَرَوْنَهُم مِّثْلَيْهِمْ رَأْىَ
15

الْعَيْنِ ط لَمْ يَلْحَقُوا بِهِم مِّنْ خَلْفِهِمْ ◀ وَإِذَا
17 ... 16

لَا تَيْنَهُم مِّن لَّدُنَّا ◀ فَامْسَحُوا بِوُجُوهِكُمْ وَأَيْدِيكُم
18

مِّنْهُ ط فَإِمَّا يَأْتِيَنَّكُم مِّنِّي هُدًى ◀ وَنَجَّيْنَهُم مِّنْ
19 ... 20

عَذَابٍ غَلِيظٍ ◀ فَوَيْلٌ لَّهُم مِّمَّا كَتَبَتْ أَيْدِيهِمْ ◀
21

وَلَمَّا يَأْتِكُم مَّثَلُ الَّذِينَ خَلَوْا ◀ قَدْ وَقَعَ عَلَيْكُمْ
23 ... 22

START DATE | PASS STAMP | TIME (MIN) | MON | TUE | WED | THU | FRI | SAT | SUN | PARENT INITIALS | CORRECTION KEY

PASS DATE

WEEK 1

WEEK 2

STRETCH LETTER ... HARAK ... JOIN

يَسْعَىٰ

FLUENCY ... PRONUNCIATION

مِّن رَّبِّكُمْ ◄ وَاِذْ نَجَّيْنٰكُمْ مِّنْ اٰلِ فِرْعَوْنَ ◄ وَمَا

وَجَدْنَا لِاَكْثَرِهِمْ مِّنْ عَهْدٍ ۚ ◄ وَقَدْ فَصَّلَ لَكُمْ مَّا

حَرَّمَ عَلَيْكُمْ ◄ اَلَّذِيْنَ يَظُنُّوْنَ اَنَّهُمْ مُّلٰقُوْا

رَبِّهِمْ ◄ نَزَعْنَا مَا فِىْ صُدُوْرِهِمْ مِّنْ غِلٍّ ◄ اَلَمْ

يُؤْخَذْ عَلَيْهِمْ مِّيْثَاقُ الْكِتٰبِ ◄ فَاَسْرِ بِعِبَادِىْ

لَيْلًا اِنَّكُمْ مُّتَّبَعُوْنَ ◄ فَهَلْ وَجَدْتُّمْ مَّا وَعَدَ

رَبُّكُمْ حَقًّا ط ◄ هُوَ الَّذِىْ خَلَقَ لَكُمْ مَّا فِى الْاَرْضِ

جَمِيْعًا ◄ مَا يُرِيْدُ اللّٰهُ لِيَجْعَلَ عَلَيْكُمْ مِّنْ حَرَجٍ ◄

وَصِيَّةً لِّاَزْوَاجِهِمْ مَّتَاعًا اِلَى الْحَوْلِ ◄ تَبْتَغُوْا

بِاَمْوَالِكُمْ مُّحْصِنِيْنَ غَيْرَ مُسٰفِحِيْنَ ◄ اَلَمْ نَسْتَحْوِذْ

عَلَيْكُمْ وَنَمْنَعْكُمْ مِّنَ الْمُؤْمِنِيْنَ ط ◄ لَوْ خَرَجُوْا فِيْكُمْ

مَّا زَادُوْكُمْ اِلَّا خَبَالًا ◄ لَنُبَوِّئَنَّهُمْ مِّنَ الْجَنَّةِ

غُرَفًا ◄ اِنَّ الَّذِيْنَ هُمْ مِّنْ خَشْيَةِ رَبِّهِمْ مُّشْفِقُوْنَ ◄

NOTES

HOMEWORK KEY		TIME (MIN)	MON	TUE	WED	THU	FRI	SAT	SUN	PARENT INITIALS	PASS STAMP		START DATE
✓	DUE	WEEK 1											
✓	PASS	WEEK 2											PASS DATE

18 C Iẓhār Shafawī (إِظْهَارشَفَوِي)

So far, I can apply the rules of:

- ✅ *Ta'awwudh* and *Basmalah*

- ✅ Mīm *Mushaddadah* and Nūn *Mushaddadah*

- ✅ *Qalqalah*

- ✅ Lām of Allāh

- ✅ *Tafkhīm*

- ✅ *Ikhfā' Shafawī*

- ✅ *Idghām Shafawī*

♥ **Iẓhār Shafawī means:**
to read the Mīm *Sākinah* clearly without *ghunnah*.

♥ **The rule is:**
if Mīm *Sākinah* appears before any other letter (i.e., other than Bā and Mīm) there will be *Iẓhār Shafawī* without *ghunnah*.

♥ **For example:**

وَيَمْنَعُوْنَ ، لَكُمْ يَلِدْ

Note:
Be careful not to do *Qalqalah* on the Mīm.

Spot the rule

Every time I see this rule, I will say:
"Mīm *Sākinah* before any other letter: *Iẓhār Shafawī*, no *ghunnah*."

NOTES

فَالْمُدَبِّرٰتِ اَمْرًا ۞ وَهُمُ الْوُفُّ ۞ اِلَّا مَا عَلَّمْتَنَا ۞
3   2   1

فَلَهُمْ اَجْرُهُمْ ۞ وَقُضِيَ الْاَمْرُ ۞ وَيُرِيكُمْ اٰيٰتِهٖ ۞
6   5   4

نَدْلُكُمْ ۞ فَيُوَفِّيهِمْ اُجُوَرَهُمْ ۞ وَاَنْعَمْتَ عَلَيْهِ ۞
9   8   7

وَلَكُمْ اَعْمَالُكُمْ ۞ فَاغْفِرْلَنَا وَارْحَمْنَا ۞ عَلٰى رَجُلٍ ۞
11   10

لَهُمْ اَجْرُهُمْ ۞ قُلْتُمْ اَنّٰى هٰذَا ۞ فَزَادَهُمْ اِيْمَانًا ۞
14   13   12

هُمْ ۞ فَصَبَّ عَلَيْهِمْ رَبُّكَ ۞ اَمْ تَسْئَلُهُمْ خَرْجًا ۞
17   16   15

اِنَّهُمْ ۞ وَبَنَيْنَا فَوْقَكُمْ سَبْعًا ۞ اَصْحٰبُ الْمَشْئَمَةِ ۞
19   18

فَوَلُّوْا ۞ تُتْلٰى عَلَيْهِمْ اٰيٰتُنَا ۞ يَكِيدُوْنَ كَيْدًا ۞
21   20

اَمْ لَمْ يَعْرِفُوْا رَسُوْلَهُمْ ۞ وُجُوْهَكُمْ شَطْرَهٗ ۞
22

وَشَاوِرْهُمْ فِى الْاَمْرِ ۞ وَقِيلَ لَهُمْ تَعَالَوْا ۞
24   23

فَاَرْسَلْنَا فِيهِمْ رَسُوْلًا ۞ فَلَكُمْ رُءُوْسُ اَمْوَالِكُمْ ۞
26   25

وَهُمْ فِى الْغُرُفٰتِ اٰمِنُوْنَ ۞ ذٰلِكُمْ اَزْكٰى لَكُمْ وَاَطْهَرُ ۞
28   27

حَاجَجْتُمْ فِيْمَا لَكُمْ بِهٖ ۞ اَوْ وَزَنُوْهُمْ ۞ وَاِذَا كَالُوْهُمْ
30   29

NOTES

عِلْمٌ ◄ رَبَّنَا وَابْعَثْ فِيهِمْ رَسُولًا ◄ يَسْـَٔلُونَكَ ¹

عَنِ الْخَمْرِ وَالْمَيْسِرِ ◄ فَاِنَّمَا هُمْ فِي شِقَاقٍ ◄ ³

فَاِنْ خِفْتُمْ اَلَّا تَعْدِلُوا ◄ لَا يَضُرُّكُمْ كَيْدُهُمْ ⁴

شَيْـًٔا ◄ يَأْكُلُونَ فِي بُطُونِهِمْ نَارًا ◄ لَكُمْ فِيهَا ⁶ ⁷

فَوَاكِهُ كَثِيرَةٌ ◄ وَلَمْ يُصِرُّوا عَلَى مَا فَعَلُوا ◄ ⁸

ثُمَّ صَرَفَكُمْ عَنْهُمْ لِيَبْتَلِيَكُمْ ◄ وَلَكُمْ نِصْفُ مَا ⁹ ¹⁰

تَرَكَ اَزْوَاجُكُمْ ◄ اِذَا فَشِلْتُمْ وَتَنَازَعْتُمْ فِي الْاَمْرِ ◄ ¹¹

وَاَرْسَلَ عَلَيْهِمْ طَيْرًا اَبَابِيلَ ○ ◄ فَاللهُ يَحْكُمُ بَيْنَهُمْ ¹²

يَوْمَ الْقِيَامَةِ ◄ ثُمَّ اِنَّكُمْ يَوْمَ الْقِيَامَةِ تُبْعَثُونَ ◄ ¹⁴

وَيَكُونُ الرَّسُولُ عَلَيْكُمْ شَهِيدًا ◄ اِنَّ اللهَ رَبِّي ¹⁵ ¹⁶

وَرَبُّكُمْ فَاعْبُدُوهُ ◄ اَلَّذِينَ هُمْ فِي صَلَاتِهِمْ ¹⁷

خَاشِعُونَ ◄ وَالْمُوفُونَ بِعَهْدِهِمْ اِذَا عَهَدُوا ◄ ¹⁸

مَثَلُهُمْ كَمَثَلِ الَّذِى اسْتَوْقَدَ نَارًا ◄ وَلَا تُلْقُوا ¹⁹ ²⁰

START DATE

PASS DATE

PASS STAMP

★

TIME (MIN) | MON | TUE | WED | THU | FRI | SAT | SUN

WEEK 1

WEEK 2

PARENT INITIALS

CORRECTION KEY

STRETCH LETTER ···· JOIN
···· HARAK
يَسْعَىٰ
FLUENCY ···· PRONUNCIATIO

NOTES

بِأَيْدِيكُمْ إِلَى التَّهْلُكَةِ ۖ ◄ فَمَهِّلِ الْكَفِرِينَ

١

أَمْهِلْهُمْ رُوَيْدًا ۞ ◄ لِيَجْمَعَنَّكُمْ إِلَى يَوْمِ الْقِيَمَةِ

٢

لَا رَيْبَ فِيهِ ◄ كَذَٰلِكَ يُبَيِّنُ اللَّهُ لَكُمْ ءَايَتِهِ ◄

٣

وَمَا تُخْفِى صُدُورُهُمْ أَكْبَرُ ۚ ◄ فَلَيْسَ عَلَيْكُمْ

٥

جُنَاحٌ أَلَّا تَكْتُبُوهَا ۗ ◄ هُوَ الَّذِى يُصَوِّرُكُمْ فِى

٦

الْأَرْحَامِ ◄ وَالَّذِينَ اتَّقَوْا فَوْقَهُمْ يَوْمَ الْقِيَمَةِ ◄

٧

حَبِطَتْ أَعْمَالُهُمْ فِى الدُّنْيَا وَالْأَخِرَةِ ۖ ◄ فَقُلْ

٨ ٩

أَسْلَمْتُ وَجْهِىَ لِلَّهِ وَمَنِ اتَّبَعَنِ ۗ ◄ إِذْ يُلْقُونَ

١٠

أَقْلَامَهُمْ أَيُّهُمْ يَكْفُلُ مَرْيَمَ ۖ ◄ فَإِنْ أُحْصِرْتُمْ

١١

فَمَا اسْتَيْسَرَ مِنَ الْهَدْيِ ۚ ◄ وَقَالُوا لِإِخْوَانِهِمْ

١٢

إِذَا ضَرَبُوا فِى الْأَرْضِ ◄ فَإِذَا دَفَعْتُمْ إِلَيْهِمْ

١٣

أَمْوَالَهُمْ ◄ تُتْلَى عَلَيْكُمْ ءَايَتُ اللَّهِ وَفِيكُمْ

١٤

رَسُولُهُ ۚ ◄ لَا تَدْرُونَ أَيُّهُمْ أَقْرَبُ لَكُمْ نَفْعًا ۚ ◄

١٥

HOMEWORK KEY	TIME (MIN)	MON	TUE	WED	THU	FRI	SAT	SUN	PARENT INITIALS	PASS STAMP	START DATE
✓ DUE	WEEK 1										PASS DATE
✓ PASS	WEEK 2										

The Prophet ﷺ *said that*

the Qur'ān will (either) plead to Allāh ﷻ on your behalf (on the Day of Judgement) and its plea is readily accepted; (or) it will be a merciless challenger whose evidence is always trusted. He who takes the Qur'ān as a leader, it will lead him to Paradise; and he who leaves the Qur'ān behind him, it will lead him to the Fire.

(Ibn Ḥibbān: 124)

19

LEVEL

19ª Qalb (قَلْب)

So far, I can apply the rules of:

✅ *Ta'awwudh* and *Basmalah*

✅ Mīm *Mushaddadah* and Nūn *Mushaddadah*

✅ *Qalqalah*

✅ *Tafkhīm*

✅ Mīm *Sākinah*

♥ ***Tanwīn*** (تَنْوِيْن)**:**
is another name for *fathatayn*, *dammatayn* and *kasratayn*.

♥ ***Qalb means:***
to change the Nūn *Sākinah* or *Tanwīn* to Mīm.

♥ ***The rule is:***
if Nūn *Sākinah* or *Tanwīn* appear before Bā, they will change to Mīm and there will be *Ikhfā' Shafawī* with *ghunnah*.

♥ ***For example:***

اٰيٰتٍ بَيِّنٰتٍ، اِذَا انْبَعَثَ

Note:
In most Qur'āns, there will be a small Mīm written above the Nūn *Sākinah* or *Tanwīn* to indicate *Qalb*.

The ghunnah here will be pronounced in the manner explained in *Ikhfā' Shafawī* (Level 18a).

Spot the rule

Every time I see this rule, I will say:
"Nūn *Sākinah* before Bā: *Qalb* with *ghunnah*"
or "Tanwīn before Bā: *Qalb* with *ghunnah*"

NOTES

أَبَدًا ◄ بِمَا ◄ بَغْيًا بَيْنَهُمْ ج ◄ فَقَالَ ائْتُوْنِيْ ◄ مِنْ

بَعْدِ مِيْثَاقِهٖ ◄ وَاَنْۢبَتَهَا نَبَاتًا ◄ صُمٌّ بُكْمٌ

عُمْىٌ ◄ مَتَاعًا بِالْمَعْرُوْفِ ◄ لَنَسْفَعًا بِالنَّاصِيَةِ ◌ ◄

وَمَنْ بَلَغَ ◄ دَعَانَا لِجَنْۢبِهٖ ◄ فَانْۢبِذْ اِلَيْهِمْ ◄ مِنْ

بَعْدِهِمْ ◄ فَاتِّبَاعٌۢ بِالْمَعْرُوْفِ ◄ يَوْمَئِذٍۭ بِجَهَنَّمَ ◄

وَاسْتَغْفِرِىْ لِذَنْۢبِكِ ج ◄ هَدْيًا بٰلِغَ الْكَعْبَةِ ◄ مِنْ

بَعْدِ مُوْسٰىﻻ ◄ سَفَهًا بِغَيْرِ عِلْمٍ ◄ زَكِيَّةًۢ بِغَيْرِ

نَفْسٍ ط ◄ مِنْ اٰيَةٍ بَيِّنَةٍ ط ◄ فَتَكُوْنُ طَيْرًاۢ بِاِذْنِىْ

فِيْهِ اٰيٰتٌۢ بَيِّنٰتٌ ◄ فِىْ كُلِّ سُنْۢبُلَةٍ ◄ اَنَّهٗ وَاقِعٌۢ

بِهِمْ ج ◄ بِسُلْطٰنٍۢ بَيِّنٍ ◄ شَهِيْدٌۢ بَيْنِىْ وَبَيْنَكُمْ

فَاِنَّهٗ فُسُوْقٌۢ بِكُمْ ط ◄ مِنْۢ بَعْدِ مَا بَيَّنَهُ ◄ حِلٌّ

بِهٰذَا الْبَلَدِ ◌ ◄ وَشَرَوْهُ بِثَمَنٍۭ بَخْسٍ ◄ هُوَ اٰخِذٌۢ

بِنَاصِيَتِهَا ◄ فَذَرُوْهُ فِىْ سُنْۢبُلِهٖ ◄ كَمَثَلِ جَنَّةٍۭ

NOTES

بِرَبْوَةٍ ◂ كَثِيرَةً بِإِذْنِ اللَّهِ ◂ إِصْلَاحٌ بَيْنَ ١

النَّاسِ ◂ إِيمَانٌ بَعْدَ إِيمَانِهِمْ ◂ وَسَبْعَ سُنْبُلَاتٍ ٣

خُضْرٍ ◂ فَبِأَيِّ حَدِيثٍ بَعْدَهُ ◂ وَتَفْرِيقًا بَيْنَ ٥

الْمُؤْمِنِينَ ◂ فَلَا تَحِلُّ لَهُ مِنْ بَعْدُ ◂ يُنْبِتُ لَكُمْ ٧

بِهِ الزَّرْعَ ◂ وَكُفْرٌ بِهِ وَالْمَسْجِدِ الْحَرَامِ ◂ تَابُوا ٩

مِنْ بَعْدِ ذَٰلِكَ ◂ فَيَكُونُ طَيْرًا بِإِذْنِ اللَّهِ ◂ مَا ١١

تَعْبُدُونَ مِنْ بَعْدِي ◂ فَأَذَّنَ مُؤَذِّنٌ بَيْنَهُمْ ١٣

فَسَالَتْ أَوْدِيَةٌ بِقَدَرِهَا ◂ وَالَّذِينَ مِنْ بَعْدِهِمْ ١٥

كُلَّ حِينٍ بِإِذْنِ رَبِّهَا ◂ وَالنُّجُومُ مُسَخَّرَاتٌ بِأَمْرِهِ ◂ ١٧

وَيَسْتَنْبِئُونَكَ أَحَقٌّ هُوَ ◂ وَمَنْ هُوَ مُسْتَخْفٍ ١٩

بِاللَّيْلِ ◂ قَلْبُهُ مُطْمَئِنٌّ بِالْإِيمَانِ ◂ يَخْرُجُ مِنْ ٢١

بُطُونِهَا شَرَابٌ ◂ وَقَفَّيْنَا مِنْ بَعْدِهِ بِالرُّسُلِ ٢٢

فَتَنْزِلَ قَدَمٌ بَعْدَ ثُبُوتِهَا ◂ بُشْرًا بَيْنَ يَدَيْ ٢٣

NOTES

رَحْمَتِهٖ ◄ ثُمَّ تَوَلَّيْتُمْ مِّنْ بَعْدِ ذٰلِكَ ◄ مَا جَعَلَ

اللّٰهُ مِنْۢ بَحِيْرَةٍ ◄ تَابُوْا مِنْۢ بَعْدِ ذٰلِكَ وَاَصْلَحُوْا

تَحْبِسُوْنَهُمَا مِنْۢ بَعْدِ الصَّلٰوةِ ◄ فَمَنْۢ بَدَّلَهٗ بَعْدَ مَا

سَمِعَهٗ ◄ مَنِ اغْتَرَفَ غُرْفَةً بِيَدِهٖ ◄ يُخْرِجُ

لَنَا مِمَّا تُنْۢبِتُ الْاَرْضُ مِنْۢ بَقْلِهَا ◄ فَاِمْسَاكٌ

بِمَعْرُوْفٍ اَوْ تَسْرِيْحٌۢ بِاِحْسَانٍ ◄ ثُمَّ يُحَرِّفُوْنَهٗ

مِنْۢ بَعْدِ مَا عَقَلُوْهُ ◄ لَوْ يَرُدُّوْنَكُمْ مِّنْۢ بَعْدِ اِيْمَانِكُمْ

كُفَّارًا ◄ ثُمَّ اتَّخَذْتُمُ الْعِجْلَ مِنْۢ بَعْدِهٖ ◄ يَوْمَ

نَدْعُوْا كُلَّ اُنَاسٍۭ بِاِمَامِهِمْ ◄ حَتّٰى تَفْجُرَ لَنَا مِنَ

الْاَرْضِ يَنْۢبُوْعًا ◌ ◄ وَاَخَذْنَا الَّذِيْنَ ظَلَمُوْا

بِعَذَابٍۭ بَئِيْسٍ ◄ فَلَعَلَّكَ تَارِكٌۢ بَعْضَ مَا يُوْحٰى

فَدَمْدَمَ عَلَيْهِمْ رَبُّهُمْ بِذَنْۢبِهِمْ فَسَوّٰىهَا ◌ ◄

اَلْيَوْمَ تُجْزٰى كُلُّ نَفْسٍۭ بِمَا كَسَبَتْ لَاظُلْمَ الْيَوْمَ ◄

19b Idghām without Ghunnah (إِدْغَامٍ)

So far, I can apply the rules of:

✓ *Ta'awwudh* and *Basmalah*

✓ Mīm *Mushaddadah* and Nūn *Mushaddadah*

✓ *Qalqalah*

✓ *Tafkhīm*

✓ Mīm *Sākinah*

✓ *Qalb*

♥ ***Idghām means:***
to merge two letters together and read them without a pause.

♥ ***The rule is:***
if Nūn *Sākinah* or *Tanwin* appear before Lām or Rā, there will be *Idghām* without *ghunnah*.

♥ ***For example:***

يَكُنْ لَّهُ ، تَوَّابًا رَّحِيمًا

Note:
In Idghām there will be no sound left from the Nūn *Sākinah* or *Tanwin* and the letter after will be read with *shaddah*.

Spot the rule

Every time I see this rule, I will say:
"Nūn *Sākinah* before Rā/Lām: *Idghām*, no *ghunnah*"
or "Tanwin before Rā/Lām: *Idghām*, no *ghunnah*"

NOTES

فَاقِعٌ ◄ مِن رَّأْسِهِ ◄ مِن رَّبِّكُمْ ◄ مِن رُّسُلِهِ ◙

مَا ◄ لِذُكُورِنَا ◄ خَالِصَةٌ لِّلنَّاسِ ◄ هُدًى ◄ لَّوْنُهَا

لِّإِثْمٍ ◄ غَيْرَ مُتَجَانِفٍ ◄ وَلٰكِن لِّيَبْلُوَكُمْ ◄ لَّمْ نُمَكِّن لَّكُمْ

مُصَدِّقًا لِّمَا مَعَكُمْ ◄ ذٰلِكُمْ خَيْرٌ لَّكُمْ ◄ اَلْحَقُّ مِن رَّبِّكَ ◄

وَاِنَّ ◄ فَهُوَ كَفَّارَةٌ لَّهُ ◙ ◄

تَفْصِيلًا ◄ وَطَعَامُكُمْ حِلٌّ لَّهُمْ ◄ كَثِيرًا لَّيُضِلُّونَ

وَلِنَجْعَلَكَ اٰيَةً ◄ بَلْ هُوَ شَرٌّ لَّهُمْ ◙ ◄ لِّكُلِّ شَيْءٍ

لٰكِن لَّعَنَهُمُ اللّٰهُ ◄ يُبَيِّنُ لَّنَا مَا لَوْنُهَا ◄ لِّلنَّاسِ

مَثَابَةً لِّلنَّاسِ ◄ فَاِن لَّمْ يَعْتَزِلُوكُمْ ◄ بِكُفْرِهِمْ

وَلَا مَوْلُودٌ لَّهُ ◄ فَاِن رَّجَعَكَ اللّٰهُ ◙ ◄ وَاٰمَنَّا ◙ ◄

فَهُوَ فِي ◄ وَلٰكِن لِّيَطْمَئِنَّ قَلْبِي ◙ ◄ بِوَلَدِهِ ◙

وَيُؤْتِ ◄ وَيْلٌ لِّكُلِّ هُمَزَةٍ لُّمَزَةٍ ○ ◄ عِيشَةٍ رَّاضِيَةٍ ○

اِنْ ◄ فَاِن لَّمْ يَكُونَا رَجُلَيْنِ ◄ مِن لَّدُنْهُ اَجْرًا ◙

NOTES

لَمۡ يَكُنۡ لَّهَا وَلَدٌ ◄ مُسَلَّمَةٌ لَّا شِيَةَ فِيهَا ◄

وَلَمۡ تَكُنۡ لَّهُ صَاحِبَةٌ ◄ فَاِنۡ لَّمۡ يَكُنۡ لَّهُ وَلَدٌ ◄

وَالۡاٰخِرَةُ خَيۡرٌ لِّمَنِ اتَّقٰى ◄ يَقُوۡلُ اَهۡلَكۡتُ مَالًا

لُّبَدًا ۝ ◄ اِنَّ فِىۡ ذٰلِكَ لَاٰيَةً لَّكُمۡ ◄ قُلۡ اِصۡلَاحٌ

لَّهُمۡ خَيۡرٌ ◄ وَتَاۡكُلُوۡنَ التُّرَاثَ اَكۡلًا لَّمًّا ◄ اِنَّ

اللّٰهَ كَانَ تَوَّابًا رَّحِيۡمًا ۝ ◄ وَلَمۡ يَكُنۡ لَّهُ كُفُوًا

اَحَدٌ ۝ ◄ يَجِدِ اللّٰهَ غَفُوۡرًا رَّحِيۡمًا ۝ ◄ وَاِنۡ لَّمۡ

تُؤۡتَوۡهُ فَاحۡذَرُوۡا ◄ وَلَلۡاٰخِرَةُ خَيۡرٌ لَّكَ مِنَ الۡاُوۡلٰى ◄

وَلَوۡ جَعَلۡنٰهُ مَلَكًا لَّجَعَلۡنٰهُ رَجُلًا ◄ لَوۡ نَعۡلَمُ قِتَالًا

لَّا اتَّبَعۡنٰكُمۡ ◄ وَلٰكِنَّ اللّٰهَ يَجۡتَبِىۡ مِنۡ رُّسُلِهٖ ◄

وَاَنَّ اللّٰهَ رَءُوۡفٌ رَّحِيۡمٌ ◄ فَجَعَلۡنٰهَا نَكَالًا لِّمَا بَيۡنَ

يَدَيۡهَا ◄ لَا تَحۡسَبُوۡهُ شَرًّا لَّكُمۡ بَلۡ هُوَ خَيۡرٌ لَّكُمۡ ◄

وَرُسُلًا لَّمۡ نَقۡصُصۡهُمۡ عَلَيۡكَ ◄ هَلۡ فِىۡ ذٰلِكَ

NOTES

قَسَمٌ لِّذِى حِجْرٍ ۝ ۞ فَاِذَا لَا يُؤْتُونَ النَّاسَ

نَقِيرًا ۝ ۞ وَلَا تَجْعَلُوا اللّٰهَ عُرْضَةً لِّاَيْمَانِكُمْ ۞

تَكُونُ لَنَا عِيدًا لِّاَوَّلِنَا وَاٰخِرِنَا ۞ وَلَا تُمْسِكُوهُنَّ

ضِرَارًا لِّتَعْتَدُوا ۞ وَاِنْ لَّمْ تَفْعَلْ فَمَا بَلَّغْتَ

رِسَالَتَهٗ ۞ وَطَعَامُ الَّذِينَ اُوتُوا الْكِتٰبَ حِلٌّ لَّكُمْ ۞

كُلُوا وَاشْرَبُوا مِنْ رِّزْقِ اللّٰهِ ۞ وَاتَّقُوا يَوْمًا

لَّا تَجْزِى نَفْسٌ عَنْ نَّفْسٍ ۞ قَالُوا ادْعُ لَنَا رَبَّكَ

يُبَيِّنْ لَّنَا مَا هِىَ ۞ فَوَيْلٌ لِّلَّذِينَ يَكْتُبُونَ الْكِتٰبَ

بِاَيْدِيهِمْ ۞ فَكَيْفَ اِذَا جَمَعْنٰهُمْ لِيَوْمٍ لَّا رَيْبَ

فِيهِ ۞ وَاَنْعَامٌ لَّا يَذْكُرُونَ اسْمَ اللّٰهِ عَلَيْهَا ۞

فَمَنْ لَّمْ يَجِدْ فَصِيَامُ شَهْرَيْنِ مُتَتَابِعَيْنِ ز

ذٰلِكَ اَنْ لَّمْ يَكُنْ رَّبُّكَ مُهْلِكَ الْقُرٰى بِظُلْمٍ ۞

فَالصّٰلِحٰتُ قٰنِتٰتٌ حٰفِظٰتٌ لِّلْغَيْبِ بِمَا حَفِظَ اللّٰهُ ۞

HOMEWORK KEY	TIME (MIN)	MON	TUE	WED	THU	FRI	SAT	SUN	PARENT INITIALS	PASS STAMP	START DATE
✓ DUE	WEEK 1										PASS DATE
✓ PASS	WEEK 2										

19 ^C Idghām with Ghunnah

So far, I can apply the rules of:

- ✓ Ta'awwudh and Basmalah

- ✓ Mīm *Mushaddadah* and Nūn *Mushaddadah*

- ✓ Qalqalah

- ✓ Tafkhīm

- ✓ Mīm *Sākinah*

- ✓ Qalb

- ✓ Idghām without ghunnah

♥ **The rule is:**

if Nūn *Sākinah* or Tanwīn appear before any of the four letters of يَنْمُوْ (ىنمرو) then Nūn *Sākinah* or *Tanwīn* will merge into the letter after them and be read with *ghunnah*.

♥ **For example:**

Note:

From here onwards, in examples like "إِنْ نَّظُنُّ" the first Nūn *Mushaddadah* should be identified as "*Idghām* with *ghunnah*" and the second one should be " Nūn *Mushaddadah, ghunnah*".

The word "*al-dunyā*" (اَلدُّنْيَا) is an exception to this rule and will not be read with *Idghām* or *ghunnah*. Details of this and other exceptions will be discussed in the Advanced Tajwīd Book.

Spot the rule

Every time I see this rule, I will say:
"Nūn *Sākinah* before Yā from يَنْمُوْ: *Idghām* with *ghunnah*"
or "Tanwīn before Yā from يَنْمُوْ: *Idghām* with *ghunnah*".

NOTES

أُمَّةً وَسَطًا ◄ إِنْ نَّظُنُّ ◄ عَامِلَةٌ نَّاصِبَةٌ ◄ ١

رَاضِيَةً مَّرْضِيَّةً ◄ وَفَاكِهَةً وَّأَبًّا ◄ وَزَيْتُونًا ٤

وَنَخْلًا ◄ مَّرْفُوعَةٍ مُّطَهَّرَةٍ ◄ وَعِنَبًا وَّقَضْبًا ٧

فِي عَمَدٍ مُّمَدَّدَةٍ ◄ مَنْ يُّفْسِدُ فِيهَا ◄ وَلَنْ يَّتَمَنَّوْهُ ٩

أَبَدًا ◄ وَمَنْ يَّكْفُرُ بِهِ ◄ اِلَى صِرَاطٍ مُّسْتَقِيمٍ ١٢

فِي صُحُفٍ مُّكَرَّمَةٍ ◄ نَّأْتِ بِخَيْرٍ مِّنْهَا ◄ خَيْرٌ مِّنْ اَلْفِ ١٤

شَهْرٍ ◄ ضَاحِكَةٌ مُّسْتَبْشِرَةٌ ◄ وَوَالِدٍ وَّمَا وَلَدَ ١٧

وُجُوهٌ يَّوْمَئِذٍ مُّسْفِرَةٌ ◄ مِنْ خَيْرٍ مِّنْ رَّبِّكُمْ ٢٠

فَضْلًا مِّنْ رَّبِّكَ ◄ وُجُوهٌ يَّوْمَئِذٍ خَاشِعَةٌ ◄ فِيهَا ٢١

سُرُرٌ مَّرْفُوعَةٌ ◄ وَاِنْ يَّأْتُوكُمْ اُسَارَى ◄ وَنَفْسٍ وَّمَا ٢٤

سَوَّاهَا ◄ يَوْمَئِذٍ يَّصْدُرُ النَّاسُ ◄ وَمَنْ يَّفْعَلْ ٢٦

ذَلِكَ ◄ وَلَكِنْ يُّؤَاخِذُكُمْ ◄ وَالْاَخِرَةُ خَيْرٌ وَّاَبْقَى ٢٨

اَيَّامًا مَّعْدُودَاتٍ ◄ اِلَّا قَلِيلًا مِّنْهُمْ ◄ اِنْ ٣٠

NOTES

نَفَعَتِ الذِّكْرَىٰ ◄ وَمِنْهُم مَّن يَقُولُ ◄ إِنَّهُ ١ ٢

لَكُمْ عَدُوٌّ مُّبِينٌ ◄ وَالٰهُكُمْ إِلٰهٌ وَاحِدٌ ◄ وَإِن ٣ ٤

يَكُن لَّهُمُ الْحَقُّ ◄ فَمَنْ خَافَ مِن مُّوصٍ ◄ وَ ٥ ٦

نَقْصٍ مِّنَ الْأَمْوَالِ ◄ فَعِدَّةٌ مِّنْ أَيَّامٍ أُخَرَ ◄ ٧

وُجُوهٌ يَوْمَئِذٍ نَّاعِمَةٌ ◄ لِنُخْرِجَ بِهِ حَبًّا وَنَبَاتًا ◄ ٨ ٩

فَإِنَّمَا هِيَ زَجْرَةٌ وَاحِدَةٌ ◄ أَإِذَا كُنَّا عِظَامًا نَّخِرَةً ◄ ١٠ ١١

فَجَعَلَهُمْ كَعَصْفٍ مَّأْكُولٍ ◄ فَأْتُوا بِسُورَةٍ مِّن مِّثْلِهِ ◄ ١٢ ١٣

وَبُرِّزَتِ الْجَحِيمُ لِمَن يَرَىٰ ◄ وَقَدْ كَانَ فَرِيقٌ مِّنْهُمْ ◄ ١٤ ١٥

وَذَٰكْثِيرٌ مِّنْ أَهْلِ الْكِتَابِ ◄ الَّذِي جَمَعَ مَالًا وَعَدَّدَهُ ◄ ١٦ ١٧

وَجَعَلْنَا سِرَاجًا وَهَّاجًا ◄ إِنَّهَا بَقَرَةٌ لَّا فَارِضٌ وَّلَا ١٨ ١٩

بِكْرٌ ◄ قَدْ عَلِمَ كُلُّ أُنَاسٍ مَّشْرَبَهُمْ ◄ لَن نَّصْبِرَ ٢٠ ٢١

عَلَىٰ طَعَامٍ وَاحِدٍ ◄ بِالْوَالِدَيْنِ إِحْسَانًا وَذِي الْقُرْبَىٰ ◄ ٢٢

وَلِكُلٍّ وِجْهَةٌ هُوَ مُوَلِّيهَا ◄ وَإِذْ قُلْتُمْ يَا مُوسَىٰ لَن ٢٣ ٢٤

نُؤْمِنَ لَكَ ◄ وَلَكُمْ فِي الْأَرْضِ مُسْتَقَرٌّ وَمَتَاعٌ ◄ فَلَا [2] [1]

جُنَاحَ عَلَيْهِ أَنْ يَّطَّوَّفَ بِهِمَا ◄ أَفْتَطْمَعُونَ أَنْ [3]

يُّؤْمِنُوا لَكُمْ ◄ عَلَيْهِمْ صَلَوٰتٌ مِّنْ رَّبِّهِمْ ◄ لَا [5] [4]

نُفَرِّقُ بَيْنَ أَحَدٍ مِّنْهُمْ ◄ لَهُ جَنَّةٌ مِّنْ نَّخِيْلٍ [6]

وَّأَعْنَابٍ ◄ وَمِنَ النَّاسِ مَنْ يَّتَّخِذُ ◄ فِيْ جِيْدِهَا [8] [7]

حَبْلٌ مِّنْ مَّسَدٍ ○ ◄ رَسُولٌ مِّنَ اللهِ يَتْلُوا صُحُفًا [9]

مُّطَهَّرَةً ◄ كَانَ النَّاسُ أُمَّةً وَّاحِدَةً ◄ فِيْهِ ظُلُمٰتٌ [11] [10]

وَّرَعْدٌ وَّبَرْقٌ ◄ الْحَجُّ أَشْهُرٌ مَّعْلُومٰتٌ ◄ وَابْعَثْ [13] [12]

فِيْهِمْ رَسُولًا مِّنْهُمْ ◄ وَمِنَ النَّاسِ مَنْ يَّشْرِيْ ◄ [14]

وَأَنْ يَّسْتَعْفِفْنَ خَيْرٌ لَّهُنَّ ◄ وَنَجِّنِيْ وَمَنْ مَّعِيَ مِنَ [16] [15]

الْمُؤْمِنِيْنَ ◄ فَسَوْفَ يُحَاسَبُ حِسَابًا يَّسِيْرًا ◄ لَهُمْ [18] [17]

نَصِيْبٌ مِّمَّا كَسَبُوا ◄ وَمَنْ يَّرْغَبُ عَنْ مِلَّةِ [19]

إِبْرٰهِمَ ◄ ذٰلِكَ تَخْفِيْفٌ مِّنْ رَّبِّكُمْ وَرَحْمَةٌ ط ◄ [20]

19d Iẓhār (إِظْهَار)

So far, I can apply the rules of:

✓ Ta'awwudh and Basmalah

✓ Mīm Mushaddadah and Nūn Mushaddadah

✓ Qalqalah

✓ Tafkhīm

✓ Mīm Sākinah

✓ Qalb

✓ Idghām without ghunnah

✓ Idghām with ghunnah

♥ **Iẓhār means:**
to read the Nūn Sākinah or Tanwīn clearly without ghunnah.

♥ **The rule is:**
if Nūn Sākinah or Tanwīn appear before any of the Six Throat Letters (ءﻫﻋﺣﻏﺧ) there will be Iẓhār and without ghunnah.

♥ **For example:**

كُفُوًا اَحَدٌ ۪ لِمَنْ خَشِيَ

Note:
An Alif that has a ḥarakah or a sukūn is also a Hamzah. Also, be careful not to do Qalqalah on Nūn.

Spot the rule

Every time I see this rule, I will say:
"Nūn Sākinah before Hamzah from ﺧﻏﺣﻫءﻋ: Iẓhār, no ghunnah"
or "Tanwīn before Hamzah from ﺧﻏﺣﻫءﻋ: Iẓhār, no ghunnah".

NOTES

كَرَّةٌ ◄ اَسِحْرُ هٰذَا ۚ ◄ نَارٌ حَامِيَةٌ ○ ◄ فَلَا تَنْهَرْ ○

خَاسِرَةٌ ○ ◄ وَلَا خَوْفٌ عَلَيْهِمْ ◄ عَبْدًا اِذَا صَلّٰى ○ ◄

مِنْ اَهْلِ الْكِتٰبِ ◄ فِيْ جَنَّةٍ عَالِيَةٍ ○ ◄ مَنْ اٰمَنَ

بِاللهِ ◄ مَتَاعًا لَّكُمْ وَلِاَنْعَامِكُمْ ◄ فَنَظِرَةٌ اِلٰى مَيْسَرَةٍ ◄

اِنَّكَ كَادِحٌ اِلٰى رَبِّكَ ◄ تَصْلٰى نَارًا حَامِيَةً ◄ وَكُلَّ

شَيْءٍ اَحْصَيْنٰهُ ◄ خَيْرٌ مِّنْ اَلْفِ شَهْرٍ ○ ◄ فَاِنْ اَسْلَمُوْا

فَقَدِ اهْتَدَوْا ۚ ◄ ذٰلِكَ لِمَنْ خَشِيَ رَبَّهٗ ○ ◄ تُسْقٰى

مِنْ عَيْنٍ اٰنِيَةٍ ◄ مَا عَلَيْكَ مِنْ حِسَابِهِمْ ◄ وَاَمَّا

مَنْ خَافَ مَقَامَ رَبِّهٖ ◄ اِلَّا مَنْ اَذِنَ لَهُ الرَّحْمٰنُ ◄ وَمَا

مِنْ اِلٰهٍ اِلَّا اللهُ ◄ بَدَّلْنٰهُمْ جُلُوْدًا غَيْرَهَا ◄ مِنْ

اَيِّ شَيْءٍ خَلَقَهٗ ○ ◄ فَصَلِّ لِرَبِّكَ وَانْحَرْ ○ ◄

اِنَّ اللهَ عَزِيْزٌ غَفُوْرٌ ◄ وَمَا مُحَمَّدٌ اِلَّا رَسُوْلٌ ◄

وَّذَّكِثِيْرٌ مِّنْ اَهْلِ الْكِتٰبِ ◄ عَلٰى شَفَا جُرُفٍ هَارٍ ◄

HOMEWORK KEY	TIME (MIN)	MON	TUE	WED	THU	FRI	SAT	SUN	PARENT INITIALS	PASS STAMP		START DATE
✓ DUE	WEEK 1											PASS DATE
✓ PASS	WEEK 2											

NOTES

وَأْتُوا الْبُيُوتَ مِنْ أَبْوَابِهَا ◄ وَلَا تُكَلَّفُ نَفْسًا اِلَّا ١

وُسْعَهَا ◄ وَأَمَّا مَنْ خَفَّتْ مَوَازِينُهُ ٢ ○ ◄ وَوُجُوهٌ ٣

يَّوْمَئِذٍ عَلَيْهَا غَبَرَةٌ ○ ◄ فَاِنْ خِفْتُمْ فَرِجَالًا اَوْ ٤

رُكْبَانًا ◄ وَكُلُوا مِنْهَا رَغَدًا حَيْثُ شِئْتُمَا ◄ فَمِنْهُمْ ٥

مَّنْ هَدَى اللهُ ◄ وَمِنْهُمْ مَّنْ حَقَّتْ عَلَيْهِ ٦

الضَّلٰلَةُ ◄ لَا تُكَلَّفُ نَفْسٌ اِلَّا وُسْعَهَا ◄ ٨

لَمْ يَلْحَقُوا بِهِمْ مِّنْ خَلْفِهِمْ ◄ يُنَادِى لِلْاِيْمَانِ ٩

اَنْ اٰمِنُوا بِرَبِّكُمْ ◄ وَمَا مِنْ حِسَابِكَ عَلَيْهِمْ ◄ ١١

فَتَرَى الْوَدْقَ يَخْرُجُ مِنْ خِلٰلِهِ ◄ وَمَا كَانَ ١٣

لِنَبِيٍّ اَنْ يَّغُلَّ ◄ اِنَّ اللهَ كَانَ عَلِيمًا حَكِيمًا ◄ ١٥

مَنْ اِلٰهٌ غَيْرُ اللهِ يَأْتِيكُمْ بِهِ ◄ لَمَا يَهْبِطُ مِنْ ١٦

خَشْيَةِ اللهِ ◄ قُلْ مَنْ حَرَّمَ زِينَةَ اللهِ ١٨

رَضِيَ اللهُ عَنْهُمْ وَرَضُوا عَنْهُ ◄ وَمَا تَفْعَلُوا مِنْ ٢٠

START DATE

PASS DATE

PASS STAMP ★

TIME (MIN)   MON   TUE   WED   THU   FRI   SAT   SUN

WEEK 1

WEEK 2

PARENT INITIALS

CORRECTION KEY

STRETCH LETTER

FLUENCY

JOIN

HARAK

PRONUNCIAT

يَسْعَى

خَيْرٍ يَّعْلَمُهُ اللهُ ◄ وَلَا طَعَامٌ اِلَّا مِنْ غِسْلِينٍ ◄

لَا يُكَلِّفُ اللهُ نَفْسًا اِلَّا وُسْعَهَا ◄ كَمَثَلِ

صَفْوَانٍ عَلَيْهِ تُرَابٌ ◄ كُلُّ شَيْءٍ هَالِكٌ اِلَّا

وَجْهَهُ ◄ مَلِكٌ يَّأْخُذُ كُلَّ سَفِيْنَةٍ غَصْبًا ◄

وَلٰكِنَّ الْبِرَّ مَنْ اٰمَنَ بِاللهِ وَالْيَوْمِ الْاٰخِرِ ◄ وَنَزَعْنَا

مَا فِيْ صُدُوْرِهِمْ مِّنْ غِلٍّ ◄ فَبَدَّلَ الَّذِيْنَ

ظَلَمُوْا قَوْلًا غَيْرَ الَّذِيْ قِيْلَ لَهُمْ ◄ وَ اللهُ يَعِدُكُمْ

مَّغْفِرَةً مِّنْهُ وَ فَضْلًا ◄ وَاِنَّ مِنَ الْحِجَارَةِ لَمَا

يَتَفَجَّرُ مِنْهُ الْاَنْهٰرُ ◄ وَاتَّقُوْا يَوْمًا لَّا تَجْزِيْ

نَفْسٌ عَنْ نَّفْسٍ ◄ وَمَا جَعَلَ عَلَيْكُمْ فِي

الدِّيْنِ مِنْ حَرَجٍ ◄ مِنْهُ اٰيٰتٌ مُّحْكَمٰتٌ هُنَّ

اُمُّ الْكِتٰبِ وَأُخَرُ مُتَشٰبِهٰتٌ ◄ اَصْحٰبُ الْجَنَّةِ

يَوْمَئِذٍ خَيْرٌ مُّسْتَقَرًّا وَّاَحْسَنُ مَقِيْلًا ○ ◄

19e Ikhfāʾ (إِخْفَاء)

So far, I can apply the rules of:

✓ *Taʿawwudh* and *Basmalah*

✓ Mīm *Mushaddadah* and Nūn *Mushaddadah*

✓ *Qalqalah*

✓ *Tafkhīm*

✓ Mīm *Sākinah*

✓ *Qalb*

✓ *Idghām* without *ghunnah*

✓ *Idghām* with *ghunnah*

✓ *Iẓhār*

♥ **Ikhfāʾ means:**

for the tip of the tongue to lightly touch the gums of the upper front teeth whilst the *ghunnah* is completed.

♥ **The rule is:**

if Nūn *Sākinah* or *Tanwīn* appear before any other letter (i.e., other than عه حء غخ and يَنْمُوْ, ر, ل, ب) there will be *Ikhfāʾ* with *ghunnah*.

♥ **For example:**

كُتُبٌ قَيِّمَةٌ , أَنْتُمْ

Note:

When pronouncing a normal Nūn or a Nūn *Mushaddadah* the tongue will press firmly against the gums. *Ikhfāʾ* is different, as the tongue will not press firmly against the gums whilst the *ghunnah* is completed.

There are fifteen letters of *Ikhfāʾ*:

ت ث ج د ذ ز س ش ص ض ط ظ ف ق ك

Spot the rule

Every time I see this rule, I will say:

"Nūn *Sākinah* before any other letter: *Ikhfāʾ* with *ghunnah*"
or "Tanwīn before any other letter: *Ikhfāʾ* with *ghunnah*"

NOTES

ءَاَنْذَرْتَهُمْ ◄ وَلَنْ تَفْعَلُوا ◄ فَاَمَّا مَنْ طَغٰى ۙ

وَكَاْسًا دِهَاقًا ۙ ◄ مِنْ كُلِّ اَمْرٍ ◄ وَلٰكِنْ ظَنَنْتُمْ

فِيْهَا كُتُبٌ قَيِّمَةٌ ◄ يَوْمَ يُنْفَخُ فِى الصُّوْرِ ◄ فَاَنْتَ عَنْهُ

تَلَهّٰى ◄ يَوْمَئِذٍ ثَمٰنِيَةٌ ◄ كَلِمَتُ فَتَابَ عَلَيْهِ ◄

يَتِيْمًا ذَا مَقْرَبَةٍ ۙ ◄ بِاَيِّ ذَنْبٍ قُتِلَتْ ۙ ◄ مِنْ شَرِّ

مَا خَلَقَ ۙ ◄ وَالْمُشْرِكِيْنَ مُنْفَكِّيْنَ ◄ قَدْ اَفْلَحَ مَنْ

زَكّٰىهَا ◄ وَكُنْتُمْ اَمْوَاتًا فَاَحْيَاكُمْ ◄ كَاَنَّ جِمٰلَتْ

صُفْرٌ ◄ فَتُصْبِحَ صَعِيْدًا زَلَقًا ◄ فِيْهَا عَيْنٌ جَارِيَةٌ

اَنْذَرْنٰكُمْ عَذَابًا قَرِيْبًا ۚ ◄ ءَاَنْتُمْ اَشَدُّ خَلْقًا ◄ اَلَمْ

يَجِدْكَ يَتِيْمًا فَاٰوٰى ◄ وَاِذَا النُّجُوْمُ انْكَدَرَتْ ۙ ◄ اِلٰى

رَبِّكَ مُنْتَهٰىهَا ۙ ◄ وَاَنْزَلْنَا مِنَ الْمُعْصِرٰتِ ◄ اَوْ مِسْكِيْنًا

ذَا مَتْرَبَةٍ ۙ ◄ سَنُقْرِئُكَ فَلَا تَنْسٰى ۙ ◄ خَيْرًا مِّنْ

جَنَّتِكَ ◄ خَلَقَكُمْ مِّنْ ضُعْفٍ ◄ فَاَنْذَرْتُكُمْ نَارًا

HOMEWORK KEY	TIME (MIN)	MON	TUE	WED	THU	FRI	SAT	SUN	PARENT INITIALS	PASS STAMP	START DATE
✓ DUE	WEEK 1 ►										PASS DATE
✓ PASS	WEEK 2 ►										

NOTES

وَإِذَا الْكَوَاكِبُ انْتَثَرَتْ ۚ ◄ وَقَدْ خَابَ مَنْ ◄ تَكَظَّىۚ

دَسَّهَا ◄ وَأَنْتَ حِلٌّ بِهَٰذَا الْبَلَدِ ۚ ◄ فَإِذَا فَرَغْتَ

فَانْصَبْ ۚ ◄ وَوَضَعْنَا عَنْكَ وِزْرَكَ ۚ ◄ وَإِنْ

جَنَحُوا لِلسَّلْمِ ◄ هٰذَا عَذَابٌ فُرَاتٌ ◄ ذِي

قُوَّةٍ عِنْدَ ذِى الْعَرْشِ ◄ وَعَمِلَ عَمَلًا صَالِحًا ◄ فَمَا

لَهُ مِنْ قُوَّةٍ وَلَا نَاصِرٍ ◄ سُورَةٌ أَنْزَلْنَاهَا وَفَرَضْنَاهَا ◄

إِنَّ الْإِنْسَانَ لَفِي خُسْرٍ ۚ ◄ فَأَنْشَرْنَا بِهِ بَلْدَةً مَيْتًا ◄

هَلْ تَرَىٰ مِنْ فُطُورٍ ◄ بَعْضُهُمْ لِبَعْضٍ ظَهِيرًا ◄

لَتَرْكَبُنَّ طَبَقًا عَنْ طَبَقٍ ۚ ◄ فَأَمَّا مَنْ ثَقُلَتْ مَوَازِينُهْ ◄

ذُرِّيَّةً ضِعَافًا خَافُوا عَلَيْهِمْ ◄ يَنْظُرُونَ مِنْ طَرْفٍ

خَفِيٍّ ◄ وَلَدَيْنَا كِتَابٌ يَنْطِقُ بِالْحَقِّ ◄ وَتُحِبُّونَ

الْمَالَ حُبًّا جَمًّا ۚ ◄ أَوَيَنْ كَذَّرَ فَتَنْفَعَهُ الذِّكْرَىٰ ۚ ◄ إِنِّي

جَاعِلٌ فِي الْأَرْضِ خَلِيفَةً ◄ أَفَلَا يَنْظُرُونَ إِلَى الْإِبِلِ ◄

START DATE

PASS DATE

PASS STAMP ★

TIME (MIN)	MON	TUE	WED	THU	FRI	SAT	SUN	PARENT INITIALS
WEEK 1								
WEEK 2								

CORRECTION KEY

JOIN
STRETCH ـ HARAKA
LETTER يَسْعَى
FLUENCY
PRONUNCIATIO

NOTES

اَلَّذِيْنَ هُمْ عَنْ صَلَاتِهِمْ سَاهُوْنَ ◄ اَرَءَيْتَ اِنْ كَذَّبَ ۱

وَتَوَلّٰى ◄ وَمَا تَخْرُجُ مِنْ ثَمَرَاتٍ ◄ فَلْيَنْظُرِ الْاِنْسَانُ ۲

مِمَّ خُلِقَ ◄ اَلَّذِيْنَ يَنْقُضُوْنَ عَهْدَ اللهِ ◄ سَيَصْلٰى نَارًا ۳

ذَاتَ لَهَبٍ ◌ ◄ قَالُوْا تِلْكَ اِذًا كَرَّةٌ خَاسِرَةٌ ◄ كُلٌّ ۸

قَدْ عَلِمَ صَلَاتَهُ وَتَسْبِيْحَهُ ◄ هٰذَا الَّذِيْ رُزِقْنَا مِنْ ۹

قَبْلُ ◄ وَاِنْ كُنْتُمْ فِيْ رَيْبٍ مِّمَّا نَزَّلْنَا ◄ اَوْ اِطْعٰمٌ فِيْ ۱۰

يَوْمٍ ذِيْ مَسْغَبَةٍ ◌ ◄ وَلَا تَشْتَرُوْا بِاٰيٰتِيْ ثَمَنًا قَلِيْلًا ◄ ۱۲

يَّوْمَ لَا تَمْلِكُ نَفْسٌ لِّنَفْسٍ شَيْئًا ◌ ◄ اِذَا دُكَّتِ الْاَرْضُ ۱۳ ۱۴

دَكًّا دَكًّا ◄ فَلْيَتَّقُوا اللهَ وَلْيَقُوْلُوْا قَوْلًا سَدِيْدًا ◄ اَنْ ۱۶ ۱۵

يَّضْرِبَ مَثَلًا مَّا بَعُوْضَةً فَمَا فَوْقَهَا ◄ وَلَمَنْ صَبَرَ ۱۷

وَغَفَرَ اِنَّ ذٰلِكَ لَمِنْ عَزْمِ الْاُمُوْرِ ◄ وَقُلْ رَّبِّ اغْفِرْ ۱۸

وَارْحَمْ وَاَنْتَ خَيْرُ الرّٰحِمِيْنَ ◄ وَقُلْ رَّبِّ ۱۹

اَنْزِلْنِيْ مُنْزَلًا مُّبَارَكًا وَّاَنْتَ خَيْرُ الْمُنْزِلِيْنَ ◄

HOMEWORK KEY	TIME (MIN)	MON	TUE	WED	THU	FRI	SAT	SUN	PARENT INITIALS	PASS STAMP	START DATE
✓ DUE	WEEK 1										PASS DATE
✓ PASS	WEEK 2										

The Prophet ﷺ said,

"Allāh ﷻ did not listen to anything in the way He listened to the Prophet ﷺ reciting the Qur'ān."
(Muslim: 792)

"Beautify the Qur'ān through your voices,
for a beautiful voice increases the Qur'ān in beauty."
(Dārimī: 3501)

20

LEVEL

20ᵃ Madd Muttaṣil (مَدّ مُتَّصِل)

So far, I can apply the rules of:

- ✅ *Ta'awwudh* and *Basmalah*
- ✅ Mīm *Mushaddadah* and Nūn *Mushaddadah*
- ✅ *Qalqalah*
- ✅ *Tafkhīm*
- ✅ Mīm *Sākinah*
- ✅ Nūn *Sākinah* & Tanwīn

♥ **The rule is:**
if a stretched letter appears before a Hamzah in the same word, I will stretch it 4 *ḥarakahs*.

♥ **For example:**

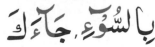

Note:
The exact lengths of the *Madds* can only be learned directly from a qualified and experienced teacher. One may find different explanations for the lengths of Madd in different books of *Tajwīd*; this is because the duration of *Madds* (4 *ḥarakahs*, 6 *ḥarakahs*, etc.) are only approximate.

As a temporary learning aid, students may open or close fingers to measure the length of *Madds*. This has been explained in the *Madd* chapter of the Safar Qā'idah.

Spot the rule

Every time I see this rule, I will say:
"Stretched letter before Hamzah in the same word: Madd Muttaṣil, 4 *ḥarakahs*."

NOTES

وَرَآءَ ظَهْرِهٖ ۙ ◄ لَوْلَا جَآءُو ◄ حَدَآئِقَ وَاَعْنَابًا ◄

٣ ٢ ١

عَلَى الْاَرَآئِكِ ◄ هُوَ قَآئِلُهَا ◄ جَزَآءً وِّفَاقًا ◄

٤ ٥ ٦

وَحَدَآئِقَ غُلْبًا ◄ وَالسَّمَآءِ وَالطَّارِقِ ◄ خُلِقَ مِنْ

٧ ٨ ٩

مَّآءٍ دَافِقٍ ◄ فَمَنْ شَآءَ ذَكَرَهٗ ◄ جَآءَتْهُمُ الْبَيِّنَةُ ◄

١١ ١٠

مِنْ سُوٓءٍ ◄ مِنْ شَعَآئِرِ اللّٰهِ ◄ لِتَكُوۡنُوۡا

١٢ ١٣ ١٤

شُهَدَآءَ ◄ يَهْدِىْ مَنْ يَّشَآءُ ◄ بَلْ جَآءَهُمْ

١٦ ١٥

بِالْحَقِّ ◄ كَمَا يَعْرِفُوۡنَ اَبْنَآءَهُمْ ◄ جَآءَكَ مِنَ الْعِلْمِ

١٨ ١٧

وَالسَّمَآءِ ذَاتِ الرَّجْعِ ◄ وَفِىْ ذٰلِكُمْ بَلَآءٌ ◄ اِنَّهَا

٢١ ٢٠ ١٩

بَقَرَةٌ صَفْرَآءُ ◄ وَالسَّمَآءِ وَمَا بَنٰهَا ◄ رِجْزًا

٢٣ ٢٢

مِنَ السَّمَآءِ ◄ وَاِذَا السَّمَآءُ كُشِطَتْ ◄ مِنْ طُوۡرِ

٢٥ ٢٤

سِيْنَآءَ ◄ اِذَا السَّمَآءُ انْفَطَرَتْ ◄ وَاَمَّا مَنْ جَآءَكَ

٢٧ ٢٦

يَسْعٰى ◄ جَزَآؤُهُمْ عِنْدَ رَبِّهِمْ ◄ اَنَّا صَبَبْنَا الْمَآءَ صَبًّا ◄

٢٩ ٢٨

اَنْ جَآءَهُ الْاَعْمٰى ◄ وَلَوِ اتَّبَعَ الْحَقُّ اَهْوَآءَهُمْ ◄ اِذَا

٣٢ ٣١ ٣٠

NOTES

السَّمَآءُ انشَقَّتْ ۟ ◂ وَادْعُوا شُهَدَآءَكُم ◂ ثُمَّ اِذَا شَآءَ ۚ 1

اَنشَرَهُ ۟ ◂ فَجَعَلَهُ غُثَآءً اَحْوَىٰ ۟ ◂ وَبَآءُو بِغَضَبٍ ۚ 3

مِّنَ اللّٰهِ ۟ ◂ اِنَّهُم هُمُ السُّفَهَآءُ ◂ اَوْ كَصَيِّبٍ مِّنَ ۚ 5

السَّمَآءِ ◂ وَاَمَّا السَّآئِلَ فَلَا تَنْهَرْ ۟ ◂ اُولٰٓئِكَ اَصْحٰبُ ۚ 7

النَّارِ ◂ وَالسَّآئِلِينَ وَفِي الرِّقَابِ ◂ فَاُولٰٓئِكَ اَتُوبُ ۚ 9

عَلَيْهِمْ ◂ وَاَدَآءٌ اِلَيْهِ بِاِحْسٰنٍ ◂ بَيْنَ السَّمَآءِ ۚ 11

وَالْاَرْضِ ◂ اُولٰٓئِكَ الَّذِينَ صَدَقُوا ◂ وَلَئِنِ ۚ 13

اتَّبَعْتَ اَهْوَآءَهُمْ ◂ تَنَزَّلُ الْمَلٰٓئِكَةُ وَالرُّوحُ ◂ اَنزَلَ ۚ 15

اللّٰهُ مِنَ السَّمَآءِ ◂ اُولٰٓئِكَ هُمْ شَرُّ الْبَرِيَّةِ ۟ ◂ اَخْرَجَ ۚ 17

مِنْهَا مَآءَهَا وَمَرْعٰهَا ۟ ◂ اُولٰٓئِكَ هُمْ خَيْرُ الْبَرِيَّةِ ۟ ◂ 19

وَاَنزَلَ مِنَ السَّمَآءِ مَآءً ◂ وَوَجَدَكَ عَآئِلًا فَاَغْنٰى ۟ ◂ 21

وَعَلَّمَ اٰدَمَ الْاَسْمَآءَ كُلَّهَا ◂ وَفُتِحَتِ السَّمَآءُ فَكَانَتْ 23

اَبْوَابًا ۟ ◂ اُولٰٓئِكَ عَلٰى هُدًى مِّن رَّبِّهِمْ ◂ وَاِلَى السَّمَآءِ 25

NOTES

كَيْفَ رُفِعَتْ ۝ وقفة ◄ يَوْمَ يَقُومُ الرُّوحُ وَالْمَلَٰٓئِكَةُ صَفًّا ◄

وَإِذْ قَالَ رَبُّكَ لِلْمَلَٰٓئِكَةِ ◄ وَلَوْ شَآءَ اللَّهُ لَذَهَبَ

بِسَمْعِهِمْ ◄ حُنَفَآءَ وَيُقِيمُوا الصَّلَٰوةَ ◄ وَجَآءَ رَبُّكَ

وَالْمَلَكُ صَفًّا صَفًّا ۝ ◄ أُو۟لَٰٓئِكَ أَصْحَٰبُ الْمَيْمَنَةِ ۝

ثُمَّ عَرَضَهُمْ عَلَى الْمَلَٰٓئِكَةِ ◄ الْفِهِمْ رِحْلَةَ الشِّتَآءِ

وَالصَّيْفِ ۝ ◄ يَسُومُونَكُمْ سُوٓءَ الْعَذَابِ ◄ إِذَا

جَآءَ نَصْرُ اللَّهِ وَالْفَتْحُ ◄ وَجِا۟ىٓءَ يَوْمَئِذٍ بِجَهَنَّمَ

جَزَآءً مِّن رَّبِّكَ عَطَآءً حِسَابًا ۝ ◄ أُو۟لَٰٓئِكَ هُمُ الْكَفَرَةُ

الْفَجَرَةُ ۝ ◄ إِنَّ الَّذِينَ كَفَرُوا سَوَآءٌ عَلَيْهِمْ ◄ وَأَنزَلْنَا

مِنَ الْمُعْصِرَٰتِ مَآءً ثَجَّاجًا ۝ ◄ يَخْرُجُ مِنۢ بَيْنِ الصُّلْبِ

وَالتَّرَآئِبِ ۝ ◄ إِلَّا ابْتِغَآءَ وَجْهِ رَبِّهِ الْأَعْلَىٰ ۝ ◄

فَمَن شَآءَ اتَّخَذَ إِلَىٰ رَبِّهِ مَآبًا ۝ ◄ ءَأَنتُمْ أَشَدُّ خَلْقًا أَمِ

السَّمَآءُ ◄ وَلَئِن سَأَلْتَهُم مَّنْ نَّزَّلَ مِنَ السَّمَآءِ مَآءً ◄

HOMEWORK KEY			

20b Madd Munfaṣil (مَدّ مُنْفَصِل)

So far, I can apply the rules of:

✅ *Ta'awwudh* and *Basmalah*

✅ Mīm *Mushaddadah* and Nūn *Mushaddadah*

✅ *Qalqalah*

✅ *Tafkhīm*

✅ Mīm *Sākinah*

✅ Nūn *Sākinah* & Tanwīn

✅ *Madd Muttaṣil*

♥ ***The rule is:***

if a stretched letter appears before a Hamzah in the next word, I will stretch it 4 *ḥarakahs*.

♥ ***For example:***

فِىٓ أَحْسَنِ، فِيهَآ أَبَدًا

Spot the rule

Every time I see this rule, I will say:

"Stretched letter before Hamzah in the next word: *Madd Munfaṣil*, 4 *ḥarakahs*."

NOTES

مَا ◀ اِلٰٓى اَجَلٍ ◀ ظَلَمُوٓا اَنْفُسَهُمْ ◀ قَالُوٓا اٰمَنَّا

فَلَا ◀ قَالَ اِنِّىٓ اَعْلَمُ ◀ قَالُوٓا اِنَّا مَعَكُمْ ◀ اَكْفُرَهٗ

وَالَّذِىٓ اَخْرَجَ ◀ خٰلِدِينَ فِيهَآ اَبَدًا ◀ اُقْسِمُ بِالشَّفَقِ

اَنَّ مَالَهٗٓ اَخْلَدَهٗ ◀ اِنَّمَآ اَنْتَ مُذَكِّرٌ ◀ الْمَرْعٰى

فَلَا ◀ مَآ اَغْنٰى عَنْهُ مَالُهٗ ◀ وَاٰتَآ اِذَا مَا ابْتَلٰىهُ

وَاٰمَنُوْا ◀ فَيَقُوْلُ رَبِّىٓ اَكْرَمَنِ ◀ اُقْسِمُ بِالْخُنَّسِ

كَلَّآ اِنَّهَا ◀ اٰمَنُوْا كَمَآ اٰمَنَ النَّاسُ ◀ بِمَآ اَنْزَلْتُ

فَيَقُوْلُ رَبِّ ◀ كَلَّا لَمَّا يَقْضِ مَآ اَمَرَهٗ ◀ تَذْكِرَةٌ

ثُمَّ اسْتَوٰٓى ◀ وَلَا يُوْثِقُ وَثَاقَهٗٓ اَحَدٌ ◀ اَهَانَنِ

لِبِثِينَ فِيْهَا ◀ لَآ اُقْسِمُ بِهٰذَا الْبَلَدِ ◀ اِلَى السَّمَآءِ

اِنَّآ اَعْطَيْنٰكَ ◀ قَالُوٓا اَتَتَّخِذُنَا هُزُوًا ◀ اَحْقَابًا

اِنَّ اللهَ اصْطَفٰٓى ◀ وَاَغْرَقْنَآ اٰلَ فِرْعَوْنَ ◀ الْكَوْثَرَ

عَلِمَتْ نَفْسٌ ◀ وَمَآ اَدْرٰىكَ مَا الطَّارِقُ ◀ اٰدَمَ

HOMEWORK KEY		TIME (MIN)	MON	TUE	WED	THU	FRI	SAT	SUN	PARENT INITIALS	PASS STAMP		START DATE
✓	DUE	WEEK 1									★		PASS DATE
✓	PASS	WEEK 2											

NOTES

مَّا أَحْضَرَتْ ۖ ◂ وَعَلَىٰٓ أَبْصَارِهِمْ غِشَاوَةٌ ۖ ◂ وَلَآ أَنَا
٢ ١

عَابِدٌ مَّا عَبَدتُّمْ ۖ ◂ لَا يُعَذِّبُ عَذَابَهُۥٓ أَحَدٌ ۖ ◂ وَمَا
٣ ٤

يَخْدَعُونَ إِلَّآ أَنفُسَهُم ◂ وَمَآ أَدْرَىٰكَ مَا الْقَارِعَةُ ۖ ◂
٥

خُذُوا مَآ ءَاتَيْنَٰكُم بِقُوَّةٍ ◂ يَجْعَلُونَ أَصَٰبِعَهُمْ فِىٓ
٦ ٧

ءَاذَانِهِمْ ◂ فَلَمَّآ أَنۢبَأَهُم بِأَسْمَآئِهِمْ ◂ وَلَا تَكُونُوٓا
٨ ٩

أَوَّلَ كَافِرٍ بِهِۦ ◂ قَالَ يَـٰٓـَٔادَمُ أَنۢبِئْهُم بِأَسْمَآئِهِمْ ◂ لَا
١٠ ١١

يَصْلَىٰهَآ إِلَّا الْأَشْقَى ۖ ◂ إِنَّآ أَنزَلْنَٰهُ فِى لَيْلَةِ الْقَدْرِ ۖ
١٢

لَمْ يَلْبَثُوٓا إِلَّا عَشِيَّةً أَوْ ضُحَٰهَا ○ ◂ وَأَوْفُوا بِعَهْدِىٓ
١٣ ١٤

أُوفِ بِعَهْدِكُمْ ◂ أَيَحْسَبُ أَن لَّمْ يَرَهُۥٓ أَحَدٌ ۖ ◂ إِنَّمَآ
١٥ ١٦

أَنتَ مُنذِرُ مَن يَخْشَىٰهَا ۖ ◂ فَتَلَقَّىٰٓ ءَادَمُ مِن رَّبِّهِۦ
١٧

كَلِمَٰتٍ ◂ إِنَّآ أَنذَرْنَٰكُمْ عَذَابًا قَرِيبًا ۖ ◂ قَالُوٓا أَنُؤْمِنُ
١٨ ١٩

كَمَآ ءَامَنَ السُّفَهَآءُ ◂ مَاذَآ أَرَادَ اللَّهُ بِهَٰذَا مَثَلًا ◂
٢٠

وَمِنْهُم مَّن يَمْشِى عَلَىٰٓ أَرْبَعٍ ◂ إِنَّهُۥ كَانَ فِىٓ
٢١ ٢٢

START DATE	PASS STAMP	TIME (MIN)	MON	TUE	WED	THU	FRI	SAT	SUN	PARENT INITIALS	CORRECTION KEY
PASS DATE	★	WEEK 1									STRETCH LETTER
		WEEK 2									FLUENCY

JOIN
HARAK
يَسْعَىٰ
PRONUNCIATI

NOTES

أَهْلِهٖ مَسْرُوْرًا ۞ ◄ وَمَآ أُمِرُوْۤا اِلَّا لِيَعْبُدُوا اللّٰهَ ◄

وَاِثْمُهُمَآ اَكْبَرُ مِنْ نَّفْعِهِمَا ◄ رَبَّنَآ اٰتِنَا فِى

الدُّنْيَا حَسَنَةً ◄ وَاِذَا دَعَوْا اِلَى اللّٰهِ وَرَسُوْلِهٖ ◄ وَمَآ

اَدْرٰىكَ مَا لَيْلَةُ الْقَدْرِ ◄ وَيٰٓاٰدَمُ اسْكُنْ اَنْتَ وَزَوْجُكَ

الْجَنَّةَ ◄ اَرْسِلْ مَعَنَا بَنِيْٓ اِسْرَآءِيْلَ ◄ فَقُلْ هَلْ لَّكَ

اِلٰٓى اَنْ تَزَكّٰى ◄ وَهُوَ الَّذِيْٓ اَرْسَلَ الرِّيٰحَ بُشْرًا بَيْنَ

يَدَيْ رَحْمَتِهٖ ◄ كَلَّآ اِذَا دُكَّتِ الْاَرْضُ دَكًّا دَكًّا ◄ فِيْۤ

اَيِّ صُوْرَةٍ مَّا شَآءَ رَكَّبَكَ ۞ ◄ وَمَا يُغْنِيْ عَنْهُ مَالُهٗۤ

اِذَا تَرَدّٰى ◄ اُذْكُرُوْا نِعْمَتِيَ الَّتِيْٓ اَنْعَمْتُ عَلَيْكُمْ ◄

وَتُوْبُوْۤا اِلَى اللّٰهِ جَمِيْعًا ◄ وَاَنْزَلْنَا فِيْهَآ اٰيٰتٍ

بَيِّنٰتٍ لَّعَلَّكُمْ تَذَكَّرُوْنَ ◄ اِنَّ اللّٰهَ لَا يَسْتَحْيٖٓ اَنْ

يَّضْرِبَ مَثَلًا ◄ شَهْرُ رَمَضَانَ الَّذِيْٓ اُنْزِلَ فِيْهِ

الْقُرْاٰنُ ◄ يٰٓاَيُّهَا الْاِنْسَانُ مَا غَرَّكَ بِرَبِّكَ الْكَرِيْمِ ◄

20^C Madd 'Āriḍ (مَدّعَارِض)

So far, I can apply the rules of:

✓ Taʿawwudh and Basmalah

✓ Mīm *Mushaddadah* and Nūn *Mushaddadah*

✓ Qalqalah

✓ Tafkhīm

✓ Mīm *Sākinah*

✓ Nūn *Sākinah* & Tanwīn

✓ Madd Muttaṣil

✓ Madd Munfaṣil

♥ **The rule is:**

if a stretched letter appears before a stopping-*sukūn*, I will stretch it 4 *ḥarakahs*.

♥ **For example:**

تَعْبُدُوْنَ ○ ٱبَابِيْلَ ○

Spot the rule

Every time I see this rule, I will say:

"Stretched letter before stopping-*sukūn*: *Madd 'Āriḍ*, 4 *ḥarakahs*."

NOTES

فَهُوَ يَهْدِينِ ۞ كَلَّا سَيَعْلَمُونَ ◄ وَطُورِ سِينِينَ ◄

وَإِيَّايَ فَارْهَبُونِ ۞ فَمَا ذَا تَأْمُرُونَ ۞ وَيْلٌ

لِّلْمُطَفِّفِينَ ۞ فَأَيْنَ تَذْهَبُونَ ۞ كِرَامًا كَاتِبِينَ ◄

يَشْهَدُهُ الْمُقَرَّبُونَ ۞ وَالْيَوْمِ الْمَوْعُودِ ۞ كَالْعِهْنِ

الْمَنفُوشِ ۞ لَكُمْ رَسُولٌ أَمِينٌ ◄ وَبِالْآخِرَةِ هُمْ

يُوقِنُونَ ۞ وَالتِّينِ وَالزَّيْتُونِ ۞ وَأُولَٰئِكَ هُمُ

الْمُفْلِحُونَ ◄ وَجَنَّاتٍ وَّعُيُونٍ ۞ فِى مَا

هُهُنَا آمِنِينَ ◄ وَلَكُمْ شِرْبٌ يَوْمٍ مَّعْلُومٍ ◄ وَلَا

تَكُونُوا مِنَ الْمُخْسِرِينَ ◄ إِنَّا مَعَكُم مُّسْتَمِعُونَ ◄

إِن كُنتُمْ صَٰدِقِينَ ۞ مِن كُلِّ زَوْجٍ كَرِيمٍ ◄

وَكَانَ مِنَ الْكَافِرِينَ ۞ مُطَاعٍ ثَمَّ أَمِينٍ ◄ ذِى

الْعَرْشِ مَكِينٍ ۞ يَعْلَمُونَ مَا تَفْعَلُونَ ۞ وَالْأَمْرُ

يَوْمَئِذٍ لِّلَّهِ ◄ عَنِ النَّبَإِ الْعَظِيمِ ۞ فِى لَوْحٍ مَّحْفُوظٍ ◄

HOMEWORK KEY	TIME (MIN)	MON	TUE	WED	THU	FRI	SAT	SUN	PARENT INITIALS	PASS STAMP		START DATE
✓ DUE	WEEK 1											PASS DATE
✓ PASS	WEEK 2											

NOTES

وَفِرْعَوْنَ ذِى الْأَوْتَادِ ۞ ◂ وَيْلٌ يَّوْمَئِذٍ لِّلْمُكَذِّبِيْنَ ۞
1 ... 2

وَارْكَعُوْا مَعَ الرَّاكِعِيْنَ ۞ ◂ قَالَ أَسَاطِيْرُ الْأَوَّلِيْنَ ۞
3 ... 4

وَالسَّمَاءِ ذَاتِ الْبُرُوْجِ ۞ ◂ فَأَرْسِلْ إِلٰى هٰرُوْنَ ۞
5 ... 6

وَهُوَ بِكُلِّ شَيْءٍ عَلِيْمٌ ◂ إِنَّهُ هُوَ التَّوَّابُ الرَّحِيْمُ ۞
7 ... 8

فَإِذَا هِيَ بَيْضَاءُ لِلنَّاظِرِيْنَ ۞ ◂ إِنَّهُ لَقَوْلُ رَسُوْلٍ
9 ... 10

كَرِيْمٍ ۞ ◂ كَلَّا بَلْ تُكَذِّبُوْنَ بِالدِّيْنِ ۞ ◂ وَلَقَدْ
12 ... 11

رَاهُ بِالْأُفُقِ الْمُبِيْنِ ۞ ◂ إِنَّكَ أَنْتَ الْعَلِيْمُ الْحَكِيْمُ ۞
13

قَالُوْا إِنَّمَا نَحْنُ مُصْلِحُوْنَ ۞ ◂ ثُمَّ إِنَّهُمْ لَصَالُوا
14 ... 15

الْجَحِيْمِ ◂ إِنَّ الْأَبْرَارَ لَفِيْ نَعِيْمٍ ۞ ◂ وَمَا أَدْرٰكَ
17 ... 16

مَا سِجِّيْنٌ ◂ لَهُمْ أَجْرٌ غَيْرُ مَمْنُوْنٍ ۞ ◂ إِنَّ بَطْشَ
19 ... 18

رَبِّكَ لَشَدِيْدٌ ◂ وَمَا صَاحِبُكُمْ بِمَجْنُوْنٍ ۞ ◂ الَّذِيْ
21 ... 20

هُمْ فِيْهِ مُخْتَلِفُوْنَ ◂ يُسْقَوْنَ مِنْ رَّحِيْقٍ مَّخْتُوْمٍ ۞
22

إِنَّ مَعِيَ رَبِّيْ سَيَهْدِيْنِ ◂ وَمِزَاجُهُ مِنْ تَسْنِيْمٍ ۞
24 ... 23

START DATE		PASS STAMP	TIME (MIN)	MON	TUE	WED	THU	FRI	SAT	SUN	PARENT INITIALS	CORRECTION KEY
		⭐	WEEK 1 ▸									STRETCH LETTER ... JOIN / HARAK
PASS DATE			WEEK 2 ▸									يَسْعٰى / FLUENCY ... PRONUNCIATIO

NOTES

اِنَّهُ هُوَ يُبْدِئُ وَيُعِيدُ ۗ وَلَا يُغْنِي مِن جُوعٍ ۙ ١

بَل هُوَ قُرْآنٌ مَّجِيدٌ ۗ وَمَآ اُرْسِلُوا عَلَيْهِمْ حٰفِظِينَ ۗ ٣

وَإِذَا مَرُّوا بِهِمْ يَتَغَامَزُونَ ۗ بَلِ الَّذِينَ كَفَرُوا ٥

يُكَذِّبُونَ ۗ بَلِ الَّذِينَ كَفَرُوا فِي تَكْذِيبٍ ۗ اِنَّ ٧

الاِنسَانَ لِرَبِّهِ لَكَنُودٌ ۗ ثُمَّ رَدَدْنٰهُ أَسْفَلَ ٩

سٰفِلِينَ ۗ الَّذِينَ طَغَوْا فِي الْبِلَادِ ۗ هَلْ ١١

اَتٰىكَ حَدِيثُ الْجُنُودِ ۗ اِنِّي اَعْلَمُ مَالَا تَعْلَمُونَ ۗ

وَمِمَّا رَزَقْنٰهُمْ يُنفِقُونَ ۗ اِن هُوَ إِلَّا الذِّكْرُ ١٤

لِلْعٰلَمِينَ ۗ يَوْمَ يَقُومُ النَّاسُ لِرَبِّ الْعٰلَمِينَ ۗ ١٥

وَإِنَّهُ لِحُبِّ الْخَيْرِ لَشَدِيدٌ ۗ اَلَيْسَ اللّٰهُ بِأَحْكَمِ ١٦

الْحٰكِمِينَ ۗ وَمَا هُوَ عَلَى الْغَيْبِ بِضَنِينٍ ۗ وَثَمُودَ ١٩

الَّذِينَ جَابُوا الصَّخْرَ بِالْوَادِ ۗ وَمَا هُوَ بِقَوْلِ شَيْطٰنٍ ٢٠

رَّجِيمٍ ۗ هَلْ ثُوِّبَ الْكُفَّارُ مَا كَانُوا يَفْعَلُونَ ۗ ٢١

HOMEWORK KEY	TIME (MIN)	MON	TUE	WED	THU	FRI	SAT	SUN	PARENT INITIALS	PASS STAMP	START DATE
✓ DUE	WEEK 1 ▶										PASS DATE
✓ PASS	WEEK 2 ▶										

20d Madd Lāzim (مَدّلَازِمٍ)

So far, I can apply the rules of:

✅ *Ta'awwudh* and *Basmalah*

✅ Mīm *Mushaddadah* and Nūn *Mushaddadah*

✅ *Qalqalah*

✅ *Tafkhīm*

✅ Mīm *Sākinah*

✅ Nūn *Sākinah* & Tanwīn

✅ *Madd Muttaṣil*

✅ *Madd Munfaṣil*

✅ *Madd 'Āriḍ*

♥ **The rule is:**
if a stretched letter appears before a *sukūn* or *shaddah*, I will stretch it 6 *ḥarakahs*.

♥ **For example:**

وَلَاالضَّآلِّينَ , آلٓمّٓ , آلْئٰنَ

Spot the rule

Every time I see this rule, I will say:
"Stretched letter before *sukūn*: *Madd Lāzim*, 6 *ḥarakahs*"
or "Stretched letter before *shaddah*: *Madd Lāzim*, 6 *ḥarakahs*".

NOTES

الٓمٓ ۚ ◄ وَالدَّوَآبُّ ◄ وَالطَّفَتِ صَفًّا ◄ غَيْرَ

مُضَآرٍّ ◄ فَمَنْ حَآجَّكَ فِيهِ ◄ قُلْ أَتُحَآجُّونَنَا

فِى اللهِ ◄ وَكُنَّا قَوْمًا ضَآلِّينَ ۞ ◄ قٓ ۚ وَالْقُرْاٰنِ

الْمَجِيدِ ۞ ◄ إِنَّ هٰٓؤُلَآءِ لَضَآلُّونَ ۞ ◄ إِذْ يَتَحَآجُّونَ

فِى النَّارِ ◄ وَإِنَّا لَنَحْنُ الصَّآفُّونَ ۞ ◄ فَإِذَا جَآءَتِ

الصَّآخَّةُ ۞ ◄ وَوَجَدَكَ ضَآلًّا فَهَدٰى ◄ وَالَّذِينَ

يُحَآجُّونَ فِى اللهِ ۞ حٰمٓ ۞ وَالْكِتٰبِ الْمُبِينِ ۞ ◄

أُدْخُلُوا فِى السِّلْمِ كَآفَّةً ۚ ◄ فَإِذَا جَآءَتِ الطَّآمَّةُ

الْكُبْرٰى ۚ ◄ لِمَ تُحَآجُّونَ فِىٓ إِبْرٰهِيمَ ◄ وَمَا هُمْ

بِضَآرِّينَ بِهِ مِنْ أَحَدٍ ◄ قُلْ أَفَغَيْرَ اللهِ تَأْمُرُوٓنِّى

وَبَثَّ فِيهَا مِنْ كُلِّ دَآبَّةٍ ۚ ◄ أَوْ يُحَآجُّوكُمْ

عِنْدَ رَبِّكُمْ ۚ ◄ وَأُولٰٓئِكَ هُمُ الضَّآلُّونَ ۞ ◄ لَا

تُضَآرَّ وَالِدَةٌۢ بِوَلَدِهَا ◄ وَلَا يُضَآرَّ كَاتِبٌ وَلَا

NOTES

شَهِيدٌ ۚ ◄ لِيُحَاجُّوكُم بِهِ عِندَ رَبِّكُمْ ۚ ◄ الٓمٓرۚ ١

تِلْكَ ءَايَٰتُ الْكِتَٰبِ ۚ ◄ وَلَآ ءَآمِّينَ الْبَيْتَ الْحَرَامَ ٢

نٓ وَالْقَلَمِ وَمَا يَسْطُرُونَ ٣ ◄ وَلَا تَحَٰضُّونَ عَلَىٰ ٤

طَعَامِ الْمِسْكِينِ ٥ ◄ ءَآللَّهُ خَيْرٌ أَمَّا يُشْرِكُونَ ٦ ◄

وَاللَّهُ خَلَقَ كُلَّ دَآبَّةٍ مِّن مَّآءٍ ۚ ◄ وَلَا تُضَآرُّوهُنَّ ٧

لِتُضَيِّقُوا عَلَيْهِنَّ ۚ ◄ ءَآلْـَٰٔنَ وَقَدْ عَصَيْتَ قَبْلُ ٨

وَكَأَيِّن مِّن دَآبَّةٍ لَّا تَحْمِلُ رِزْقَهَا ۚ ◄ الٓرۚ تِلْكَ ٩ ١٠

ءَايَٰتُ الْكِتَٰبِ الْمُبِينِ ٠ ◄ وَلَيْسَ بِضَآرِّهِمْ شَيْـًٔا ١١ ١٢

إِلَّا بِإِذْنِ اللَّهِ ۚ ◄ لَمْ يَطْمِثْهُنَّ إِنسٌ قَبْلَهُمْ وَلَا ١٣

جَآنٌّ ٠ ◄ فَاذْكُرُوا اسْمَ اللَّهِ عَلَيْهَا صَوَآفَّ ۚ ١٤

وَمَا كَانَ الْمُؤْمِنُونَ لِيَنفِرُوا كَآفَّةً ۚ ◄ طٰسٓمٓ ٠ تِلْكَ ١٥ ١٦

ءَايَٰتُ الْكِتَٰبِ الْمُبِينِ ٠ ◄ فَتَحْرِيرُ رَقَبَةٍ مِّن قَبْلِ ١٧

أَن يَتَمَآسَّا ◄ وَخَلَقَ الْجَآنَّ مِن مَّارِجٍ مِّن نَّارٍ ◄ ١٨

NOTES

ذٰلِكَ بِاَنَّهُمْ شَآقُّوا اللّٰهَ وَرَسُولَهٗ ◄ مَا مِنْ [1]

دَآبَّةٍ اِلَّا هُوَ اٰخِذٌۢ بِنَاصِيَتِهَا ط ◄ فَاِنْ حَآجُّوكَ [2]

فَقُلْ اَسْلَمْتُ وَجْهِيَ لِلّٰهِ ◄ وَاِنْ يَّرُدْكَ بِخَيْرٍ [3]

فَلَا رَآدَّ لِفَضْلِهٖ ط ◄ وَاِنْ كُنْتُمْ مِّنْ قَبْلِهٖ لَمِنَ [4]

الضَّآلِّيْنَ ۟ ◄ وَمَنْ يَّقْنَطُ مِنْ رَّحْمَةِ رَبِّهٖۤ اِلَّا [5]

الضَّآلُّوْنَ ۟ ◄ اَلَمْ تَرَ اِلَى الَّذِيْ حَآجَّ اِبْرٰهٖمَ [6]

فِيْ رَبِّهٖۤ ◄ آلْـٰٔنَ ◄ وَقَدْ كُنْتُمْ بِهٖ تَسْتَعْجِلُوْنَ ◄ [7]

اَلْحَآقَّةُ ۟ مَا الْحَآقَّةُ ۟ وَمَاۤ اَدْرٰىكَ مَا الْحَآقَّةُ ۟ [8]

قَالُوْا لَبِثْنَا يَوْمًا اَوْ بَعْضَ يَوْمٍ فَسْـَٔلِ الْعَآدِّيْنَ ۟ [9]

فَيَوْمَىِٕذٍ لَّا يُسْـَٔلُ عَنْ ذَنْۢبِهٖۤ اِنْسٌ وَّلَا جَآنٌّ ۟ [10]

اَوَلَمْ يَرَوْا اِلَى الطَّيْرِ فَوْقَهُمْ صٰٓفّٰتٍ وَّيَقْبِضْنَ ۘ مَ [11]

وَلَا تَتَّبِعٰٓنِّ سَبِيْلَ الَّذِيْنَ لَا يَعْلَمُوْنَ ۟ ◄ [12]

غَيْرِ الْمَغْضُوْبِ عَلَيْهِمْ وَلَا الضَّآلِّيْنَ ۟ ◄ [13]

20^e Madd Aṣlī (مَدّ أَصْلِي)

So far, I can apply the rules of:

- ✅ *Ta'awwudh* and *Basmalah*

- ✅ Mīm *Mushaddadah* and Nūn *Mushaddadah*

- ✅ *Qalqalah*

- ✅ *Tafkhīm*

- ✅ Mīm *Sākinah*

- ✅ Nūn *Sākinah* & Tanwīn

- ✅ *Madd Muttaṣil*

- ✅ *Madd Munfaṣil*

- ✅ *Madd 'Āriḍ*

- ✅ *Madd Lāzim*

♥ **The rule is:**

if a stretched letter appears before anything else (i.e., other than Hamzah, *sukūn* and *shaddah*), I will stretch it 2 ḥarakahs.

♥ **For example:**

ٱئْتُونِي ، نُوحِيهَا

Note:

A detailed explanation of *Madd Aṣlī* can be found in Safar Qā'idah, Level 6, under the title "Stretched Ḥarakahs".

Spot the rule

Every time I see this rule, I will say:

"Stretched letter before anything else: *Madd Aṣlī*, 2 ḥarakahs."

NOTES

فَتَمَتَّعُوا وقفة ◄ فَانْظُرُوا ◄ وَكَانُوا شِيَعًا ◄ فَتُثِيرُ ¹

سَحَابًا ◄ وَيَجْعَلُهُ كِسَفًا ◄ وَأَقِمِ الصَّلوٰةَ ◄ وَاللّٰهُ ⁴

يَقُولُ الْحَقَّ ◄ خٰلِدِينَ فِيهَا ◄ مُنِيبِينَ اِلَيْهِ ◄ ⁷

وَلَا تَخُطُّهُ بِيَمِينِكَ ◄ وَيُؤْتُونَ الزَّكوٰةَ ◄ فَذُوقُوا ¹⁰

بِمَا نَسِيتُمْ ◄ فَجَاءُوهُمْ بِالْبَيِّنٰتِ ◄ وَذَكَرَ اللّٰهَ كَثِيرًا ¹²

ذٰلِكَ الدِّينُ الْقَيِّمُ ◌ ◄ فِي بِضْعِ سِنِينَ ◄ وَكَفٰى ¹⁵

بِاللّٰهِ وَكِيلًا ⃝ ◄ اُذْكُرُوا نِعْمَةَ اللّٰهِ ◄ بَلْ هُوَ اٰيٰتٌ ¹⁸

بَيِّنٰتٌ ◄ وَسَبِّحُوا بِحَمْدِ رَبِّهِمْ ◄ اِنَّ بُيُوتَنَا عَوْرَةٌ ²⁰

مَا لَبِثُوا غَيْرَ سَاعَةٍ ◄ وَلِتَبْتَغُوا مِنْ فَضْلِهِ ◄ وَ ²²

نَحْنُ لَهُ مُسْلِمُونَ ◄ فَاِذَا رَكِبُوا فِي الْفُلْكِ ◄ اُتْلُ ²⁵

مَا اُوحِيَ اِلَيْكَ ◄ سِيرُوا فِي الْاَرْضِ ◄ وَاتَّقُوهُ ²⁷

وَاَقِيمُوا الصَّلوٰةَ ◄ لَا مَقَامَ لَكُمْ فَارْجِعُوا ◄ فَاٰتِ ²⁹

ذَا الْقُرْبٰى حَقَّهُ ◄ يُولِجُ الَّيْلَ فِي النَّهَارِ ◄ وَالْهُنَا ³¹

NOTES

وَالْهُكُمْ وَاحِدٌ ◂ فَاِنَّكَ لَا تُسْمِعُ الْمَوْتٰى ◂ اِنَّهٗ لَا ¹

يُحِبُّ الْكٰفِرِيْنَ ○ اَللّٰهُ بَرْزُقُهَا وَاِيَّاكُمْ ◂ لَا ³

تَبْدِيْلَ لِخَلْقِ اللّٰهِ ◂ وَلِيُنْذِيْقَكُمْ مِّنْ رَّحْمَتِهٖ ◂ ⁵

ثُمَّ يُمِيْتُكُمْ ثُمَّ يُحْيِيْكُمْ ◂ نَخَافُوْنَهُمْ كَخِيْفَتِكُمْ ⁷

اَنْفُسَكُمْ ◂ مِنَ الَّذِيْنَ فَرَّقُوْا دِيْنَهُمْ ◂ تَنْهٰى عَنِ ⁸ ⁹

الْفَحْشَاءِ وَالْمُنْكَرِ ◂ يَعْلَمُ مَا فِي السَّمٰوٰتِ وَالْاَرْضِ ◂ ¹⁰

وَصَاحِبْهُمَا فِي الدُّنْيَا مَعْرُوْفًا ◂ وَلَقَدْ اَرْسَلْنَا مِنْ ¹¹ ¹²

قَبْلِكَ رُسُلًا ◂ اِذَآ اَذَا قَهُمْ مِّنْهُ رَحْمَةً ◂ وَاتَّبِعْ ¹³ ¹⁴

سَبِيْلَ مَنْ اَنَابَ اِلَيَّ ◂ فَانْتَقَمْنَا مِنَ الَّذِيْنَ ¹⁵

اَجْرَمُوْا ◂ ثُمَّ اِذَا دَعَاكُمْ دَعْوَةً ◂ وَاَثَارُوا ¹⁶ ¹⁷

الْاَرْضَ وَعَمَرُوْهَا ◂ اَللّٰهُ يَبْدَؤُا الْخَلْقَ ثُمَّ يُعِيْدُهٗ ◂ ¹⁸

وَاخْتِلَافُ اَلْسِنَتِكُمْ وَاَلْوَانِكُمْ ◂ سُبْحٰنَهٗ وَتَعٰلٰى ¹⁹ ²⁰

عَمَّا يُشْرِكُوْنَ ○ وَيَقُوْلُوْنَ مَتٰى هٰذَا الْفَتْحُ ◂ ²¹

START DATE

PASS DATE

PASS STAMP

★

TIME (MIN) | MON | TUE | WED | THU | FRI | SAT | SUN

WEEK 1 ▸

WEEK 2 ▸

PARENT INITIALS

CORRECTION KEY

STRETCH LETTER
FLUENCY

JOIN
HARAF

يَسْعٰى

PRONUNCIAT

NOTES

وَلَا تُطِعِ الْكَفِرِينَ وَالْمُنَفِقِينَ ۗ إِنَّ اللَّهَ عِنْدَهُ

عِلْمُ السَّاعَةِ ۚ فَإِخْوَانُكُمْ فِى الدِّينِ وَمَوَالِيكُمْ ۚ

ثُمَّ سَوَّىٰهُ وَنَفَخَ فِيهِ مِن رُّوحِهِ ۚ وَأَخَذْنَا مِنْهُم

مِّيثَاقًا غَلِيظًا ۝ لَآتَيْنَا كُلَّ نَفْسٍ هُدَىٰهَا

نَاكِسُوا رُءُوسِهِمْ عِنْدَ رَبِّهِمْ ۗ أَوَلَمْ يَرَوْا أَنَّا

جَعَلْنَا حَرَمًا ءَامِنًا ۚ وَلَا يَأْتُونَ الْبَأْسَ إِلَّا قَلِيلًا

وَقِيلَ لَهُمْ ذُوقُوا عَذَابَ النَّارِ ۚ فَأَرْجِعْنَا نَعْمَلْ

صَالِحًا إِنَّا مُوقِنُونَ ۝ وَقَالُوٓا أَءِذَا ضَلَلْنَا فِى

الْأَرْضِ ۚ فَأَرُونِى مَاذَا خَلَقَ الَّذِينَ مِن دُونِهِ ۚ

إِنَّ أَنسَيْنَكُمْ وَذُوقُوا عَذَابَ الْخُلْدِ ۚ لَا يَنْفَعُ الَّذِينَ

ظَلَمُوا مَعْذِرَتُهُمْ ۚ يَتَوَفَّىٰكُمْ مَّلَكُ الْمَوْتِ الَّذِى

وُكِّلَ بِكُمْ ۚ أَنَّا نَسُوقُ الْمَآءَ إِلَى الْأَرْضِ

الْجُرُزِ ۚ وَعَلَى اللَّهِ فَلْيَتَوَكَّلِ الْمُؤْمِنُونَ ۝

The Prophet ﷺ said,

"Surely this Qur'ān is the banquet of Allāh, so take from His banquet whatever you are able to. No doubt, this Qur'ān is the rope of Allāh, the clear light, the beneficial cure, a protection for the one who holds on to it and salvation for the one who follows it."

(Ḥākim:2040)

ILLUSTRATED
ISLAMIC STUDIES SERIES

We've honed our Islamic Studies syllabus with more than a decade of practical feedback from teachers and students from across the UK.

With content ranging from the stories of the Prophets to contemporary 21st Century issues, these beautifully illustrated books blend traditional Islamic Sciences and modern educational teaching methods to enhance learning.

Authentic
Islamic knowledge
Fun, simple and engaging
Age appropriate content
Associated workbooks
Teacher training &
Resources

 ORDER ONLINE AT **SAFARPUBLICATIONS.ORG**

LEARN BY HEART SERIES
Essential Duas & Surahs

Authentic duas
Estimated learning time
Virtues of duas included
Tried and tested
Progress trackers
Clear and simple layout

online